Unlocking the Secrets of E-Book Publishing

Get your books into effective sales channels (with or without Amazon)

By Doris Elaine Booth

First Authorlink® Edition, 2017

Copyright© 2016-2017 by Doris E. Booth

ISBN: 978-1-928704-57-7 (EPUB)

ISBN: 978-1-928704-58-4 (Mobi)

ISBN: 978-1-928704-59-1 (Print)

Cover Artist: Vanessa Sanoja

www.authorlink.com

Dedication

I dedicate this book to my dear friends and colleagues,
Elaine Lanmon and Linda Lee
who have given their full creative support to this effort — Elaine with her
artistic skills in design and layout, and Linda with her expertise in line
editing and grammar. Special thanks for all the feedback and help from
William Kowalski, Patrick LoBrutto, Nathan Pabst, Lloyd Jassin,
and to Craig Mewbourne and his team at Empathy Alpha.
This work is for all the authors who need
to understand and navigate through the rough seas of self-publishing.

Introduction

So, you are about to publish a book in both e-book and/or print-on-demand formats. Now, what?

How will you get your baby out into the world? So many publishing services offer to design, produce and/or distribute your work. How do you know you are choosing the right services? Is Amazon Kindle's enticing 70% royalty plan really the best avenue for you, or are there better ways to get your book into the wider marketplace?

What appears as an appealing way of distributing your book may not yield the best financial results.

Part One of the book provides some practical tools for getting your work as a self-published author into major sales channels. **Part Two** offers a deeper look at the giant retailer, Amazon.com, and examines how that venue may or may not be the most effective distribution outlet for you.

The digital book landscape is fraught with logistical and technical complexities, as well as outright scams. One of your biggest challenges as a self-published or small press author is to get savvy about how and where your work is available for sale in the marketplace. That will involve:

- knowing how to structure your book to improve its discoverability
- how royalty plans actually will impact your earnings
- how various publishing services differ
- knowing where your book will be distributed and sold
- awareness of obscure restrictions that can trip you up.

In the old days, your publisher handled all the distribution aspects of your book. Today, as a self-published author it is all up to you.

The focus of this book is to give you the tools for do-it-yourself distribution. The emphasis is on online e-book and print-on-demand (POD) book distribution through US retailers with domestic and foreign distribution partnerships.

In pure industry terms, publishing, promotion, and distribution are three very different things. Today, we can loosely refer to distribution as "publishing services," because the job of distribution now includes many aspects.

"**Publishing**" is the process of making the book ready to release. These days some of that work may be performed by a publishing service, or an online retailer offering certain automated tools.

"**Promotion**" is how you make the work visible to potential audiences and convince them to buy. The way you prepare your files for distribution can help influence the visibility of the book.

"**Distribution**" is the mechanism by which you deliver your books through the various sales channels and into hands of your readers. Today this requires that you "convert" your manuscript to one or more digital files that can be "read" and sold by various retailers such as Amazon and/or Barnes & Noble.

Without efficient distribution, the other two activities — publishing and promotion — are pretty useless. It's not enough to upload your book to say, Amazon and expect the royalties to roll in.

Designing an adequate distribution plan (as opposed to working with an actual distributor) takes a little work. In fact, it can get pretty laborious. Retailers don't like to tell you that because they want you to upload more and more content so they can appear bigger and bigger to their audiences, and make shiploads of money, while you starve on your dreams. In other words, they are not necessarily your best friends.

We hope that this content will give you a solid basis for getting the widest distribution for your book while avoiding some nasty bumps in the road.

Here we will concentrate on distribution for the self-published author who wants to deliver in both e-book and small-quantity print formats through what is known as author portals or self-serve publishing sites.

We endeavor to strip away the slick marketing ploys of several major retailers to give you a truer picture of the e-book and POD distribution world.

We have used our best efforts to present timely and accurate information on the distribution process. However, technology, retail outlets and e-book production techniques are changing rapidly. We urge the reader to check the latest guidelines for any and all stores and distributors before signing any publisher agreement. The lists of the main restrictions posted here, for example, do not include all constraints.

This book provides an overview to help you think about the challenges you will face in self-distribution. Each decision you make along the way will be important to your success.

What Method Will You Use?

Traditional online publisher accounts are usually only available to those who have 100 titles or more to distribute. Smaller publishers now have two main ways to distribute their work.

1. Do-it-yourself setup of your own publishing accounts with retailers. Using retailers as direct distribution services can save you time, money and give you greater control over your products.

2. Pick an **aggregator** (a third party that bundles many services together), or a traditional distributor. This approach can be marginally easier, but expensive and can be fraught with hidden conditions. When you are choosing a distribution method, consider how:
   - pricing rules of a retailer might impact your income
   - exclusivity and termination clauses can work against you
   - content creation tools can box you in to exclusivity
   - unclear fees can eat into your royalties
   - some royalty rates are designed to bait you, and they look better than they really are.

Some Initial Steps

- First survey the possible sales channels to determine which channels might best fit your book(s) and give you the most visibility (later chapters will get you started).

- Be aware that if you pick an exclusive plan with any retailer, you are limiting your opportunity to sell the book anywhere else, not even on your own web site. Exclusivity could limit your income as well as your visibility. The plan(s) you choose must serve your overall goals.

- If you have decided to go with non-exclusive royalty plans at several retailers, you will need to avoid sales channel conflicts or duplication. Conflict occurs if, in a non-exclusive arrangement, two or three retailers wind up feeding the same book title to the same sub-sites in their customer network. If vendor A is selling to some of the same outlets as vendor B under two different stock-keeping numbers (or ISBN's), things can get pretty messy and may cause you to be kicked out of a sales channel. To avoid both types of conflict, retailers have certain "opt out" terms in their sign-up agreements. For example, when you first set up your account and fill out the legal agreements with IngramSpark, you can "**opt out**" of Kindle if you already have an Amazon deal. Since

Ingram and Amazon have some mutual sales outlets, this option insures your book won't appear on the same reseller site under two different stock numbers.

- Lastly, in this fast-changing environment, read the retailer's specifications and all the fine print, especially if you are using a third-party middle man to distribute your books. Some aggregators — those whose sales outlets may include the same ones being fed by other retailers — can't distribute your title at all if it's already in another channel. You may not realize this until you have spent a lot of money or signed an agreement with such an aggregator.

A Word About ISBN Numbers and Formats

Our focus for this book is on distribution, rather than design and production of an e-book. But one needs a basic understanding of **ISBN** numbers and e-book formats before launching into self-distribution.

ISBN

An International Standard Book Number (ISBN) is a unique identifier that helps book purveyors world-wide locate your book, know the author's name and what the book is about. Without an ISBN you will not be found in many book stores, online or down the street from your house. Bowker is the leading provider of bibliographic data such as ISBN numbers, and your titles are exposed to many facets of the book industry through this single web application. You can register your titles and get ISBN's at Bowker My Identifier Services[1] or another service. Among others are Publisher Services[2], ISBN Agency[3], and ISBN Services[4]. However, Bowker is by far the preferred registrar. The service is the leading provider of bibliographic data for libraries and booksellers. Thus your titles are exposed to a wide audience of book buyers.

The Purpose of ISBN Numbers, and Why You Need One

The purpose of the ISBN is to identify one specific version of a book. Most retailers require, or at least prefer, that you have an ISBN number for your book, even if they assign their own stock-keeping number to your title.

---

[1] https://www.myidentifiers.com/isbn/main
[2] http://www.isbn-us.com/home1/?gclid=CNPvl6aivMsCFQwxaQodTmMDKA
[3] http://www.isbnagency.com/
[4] http://www.isbnservices.com/product/basic-isbn-number-barcode/?gclid=CMjn5fSivMsCFQcLaQodjcwJJA

If you wish to have a hard bound copy, a softbound copy, an **EPUB**, a **PDF**, a **MOBI**, or even if you register a new version, it is the best industry practice to have a unique ISBN for each version. A unique identifier enables retailers to help the customer understand which exact version of a title they are purchasing. Currently, there are 13 numbers in an ISBN. Older books may have nine or ten digits, but are no longer acceptable, unless grand-fathered into the system.

The numbers have a specific meaning. The current ISBN-13 will be prefixed by "978." Next will be an identifier for a geographical group of publishers, such as the USA. Next is the number or numbers that identify the publisher within the geographic group, then the title identifier which identifies the particular title or edition, and last, the check digit, a single number at the end of the ISBN used by computer systems to validate numbers-checking against errors in transcription.

Ideally, you need an ISBN number for each format of the book — one for the EPUB, one for the Kindle Mobi, one for the print book and so on.

To avoid producing a different version of the book's interior for each ISBN, you can list all of the unique identifiers on the copyright page of your book by placing the format in parentheses, something like this:

ISBN 978-192XXXX-000 (EPUB)
ISBN 978-192 XXXX -001 (Mobi)
ISBN 978-192XXXX-003 (Print)

Thus, the copyright page of your master file will not have to be changed for each format, and can alert people that other formats are available.

Tip: Amazon doesn't require an ISBN to list your book on their website, but Apple does. Amazon assigns its stock-keeping number to your title when uploaded through its publishing portal.

Remember, the ISBN is not only unique to the book title, but also to the publisher. If a publishing service offers you a free ISBN, that number might forever identify your title as being published by that particular service rather than by you. Beware of a publishing service or ISBN sales reseller that assigns you an ISBN from a large block of numbers it has acquired from a real ISBN service such as Bowker. Read the fine print to assure that the ISBN you buy will list you as the publisher, and not someone else.

Formats

A "**format**" is simply the way something is arranged or laid out. If this section boggles your mind, simply skip the material. In many cases, you don't need to know much about formats, but it's always good to be able to converse with vendors with a basic understanding of the technical aspects of the e-book production task.

A manuscript must be transformed into a particular e-book (or digital) format before a major retailer will accept the work. Generally, you cannot just upload your Word document or PDF directly for sale to most retail stores. It must go through a "conversion" process that adds programming code to the file, called Extensible Markup Language (**XML**) This markup language defines a set of rules for encoding documents in a format that is both human-readable and machine-readable.

Why is XML needed? A traditional printed book holds its form and page layout whether it appears on the bookshelf at a store, like Barnes & Noble, or the local bookshop on the corner. No matter where the printed book is transported, it looks the same. Not so for e-books. E-books (or digital books) are real "shape shifters" — like the mythical characters who can change their physical form or identity to suit their surroundings or to please another person.

The following discussion tells you a little about how e-book formats work and also why.

E-books are fluid (even in the case of so-called "fixed formats", which we will discuss). The e-book format can pour its contents into many different vessels which in this case are numerous smartphones and reading devices.

What gives an e-book capacity to change its shape? Answer: XML-based computer programming code that lies hidden inside the computer file and tells the pages how to behave no matter what device displays them.

The programming code in your book file must know how to talk to the programs (and devices) which retailers have built into their store software and applications. And each retailer has slightly different specifications for how they want those files programmed. Some retailers don't like sharing files with other vendors, so they create proprietary (secret) dialects of their own, such as the Mobi format, which is exclusive to Amazon Kindle. Your book must then speak their dialect (if not their language) to be accepted into that retailer's store.

If you work with a consultant or an aggregator (a third-party who puts all the pieces of the process together for you), you may not need to know the inner-workings of an e-book, but having a cursory understanding of what is involved can make it easier for you to work with them. If you are not interested in knowing what's under the hood of e-books, just skip to Chapter One — though some of this information may be relevant to you. In either case, don't worry. There are plenty of folks and tools out there to help you through the process. Here are the main e-book file formats:

EPUB is a standard format for open e-books maintained by the International Digital Publishing Forum[5] (**IDPF**. An EPUB is a group of files zipped together into a single package, which ends in the extension, EPUB.

When you unzip an EPUB 3, you see one file and two folders:
- File: Mimetype
- Folders: META-INF and OEBPS

The **META-INF folder**, which contains the book's metadata information (description), can contain one or multiple files, but it must contain a container.Xml file. This file tells the vendor or retailer how to process the rest of the EPUB package.

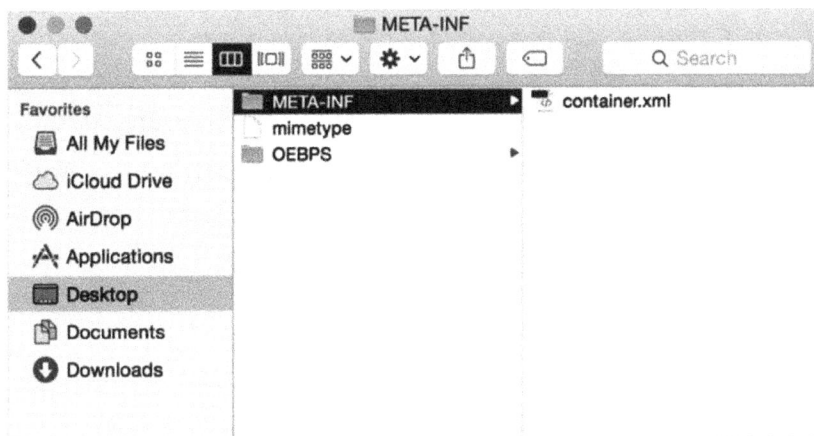

Figure 1. Meta-INF

The OEBPS folder* contains the book's content, metadata, style, and table of contents.

---

[5] http://idpf.org/

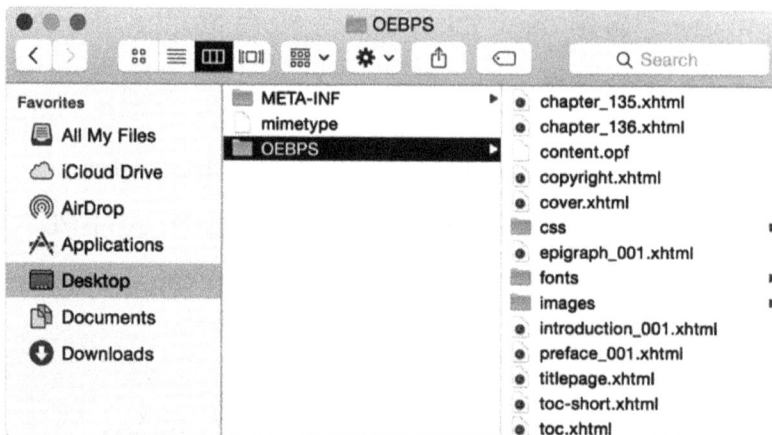

Figure 2. Meta-INF

In the OEBPS folder, you must include these files:

- **XHTML** files for your content, which can include text, images, and media. The table of contents, a navigation file, is often named toc.XHTML.

- A file named content.Opf, which describes the metadata, the manifest (what files are in the OEBPS folder) and the display order of those files.

You can also include a cascading style sheet (CSS) in the OEBPS folder to describe the styling and layout of the book. You don't necessarily need to know the inner-workings of digital files to publish your book. Many production tools and consulting companies are available. These basics will help you know what questions to ask your production team.

Preparing Your File for Digital Distribution Is Key

Most author portals (points of distribution) have a means to help you upload your manuscript for sale on their site. Despite these simplified tools, the process can be challenging, especially since each vendor's requirements vary. EPUB usually serves as the "base" file from which other formats are created, such as rendering the file into Mobi for Amazon Kindle or an optimized version of EPUB for distribution on Apple devices. After you carefully read each vendor's instructions for preparing your manuscript for publication, and once you have an EPUB file in hand, we strongly suggest you check your file for errors by running the finished document through the International Digital Publishing Forum (IDPF) **EPUB validator**[6], sometimes called **EPUBChecker.**

Validating your e-book's technical accuracy is as important as proofreading for grammatical and spelling errors. Not only will validation ensure your book looks good and performs as intended, but if the work does not meet the technical requirements of the vendor, the title will be suppressed from being seen or sold on a retail site. Fixing mistakes after the

---

[6] http://validator.idpf.org/

book has been placed into sales channels can be very complicated and costly.

E-book production per se is a subject for another book, and there are numerous formats, some including audio and video. It is useful to know the names of the five most popular e-book formats:

1. **EPUB 2 or 3 Standard** (reflowable)
2. EPUB fixed layout
3. iBook for Apple
4. Kindle Fire (Amazon Kindle's more advanced programming)
5. Mobipocket (older programming for Kindle)

Different retail distributors accept different formats. They also have their proprietary software tools that can be used to generate an e-book format which can then be uploaded to their store. Most of these specialized tools are useful only for the simplest books. Complicated ones may require a professional conversion house.

The trouble with the retailer tools is that they are often exclusive to the retail store which hosts the tool. Apple, for example, has two such programs — iTunes Producer and iBook Author. If you use iTunes Producer for preparing and submitting your e-book to Apple, the file can only be used and sold in the Apple store and nowhere else (unless you know how to hack the system). On the other hand, if you decide not to submit your book for sale in the iBooks Store[7], you can use Apple's iBook Author to create a book file that you can distribute yourself. You can also export your book as a PDF file, which can be viewed or printed using Preview, Adobe Reader or any PDF reader application. Links work in the exported PDF, but other interactive media, such as movies or 3-D probably will not function well.

Main E-Book Formats
in Use Today

EPUB Standard

The **standard EPUB** format uses the simplest form of programming to display a book on a smartphone or reading device and is suitable only for documents that are almost all text. The format is described as "**reflowable**" because the text flows from page to page as if pouring the content like water. The reflowable format makes the text readable on many different devices, but with little control over design, other than paragraphs and page breaks. Books that have many images, multiple columns or graphical design are not appropriate for

---

[7] http://support.apple.com/kb/PH2827?viewlocale=en_US&locale=en_US

reflowing text. It is also the least expensive format to produce. The reflowable format cannot accurately reproduce the look of a printed book.

EPUB Fixed Layout (FXL)

Fixed layout is a more sophisticated format for illustrated or very complex books with many images, columns, charts and graphs.

This format is popular for children's e-books[8] and complex non-fiction like cookbooks and textbooks. Unlike standard e-book files[9] fixed layout e-books can keep the same page layout and design as their print book counterparts and can sometimes contain audio or video enhancements that make them more interactive.

Fixed Layout e-books are not PDFs. They are fully-functional HTML-based e-book files.

The fixed layout forces the device upon which it is displayed to render differently than if it were simply re-flowable.

---

[8] http://ebookarchitects.com/learn-about-ebooks/childrens-ebooks/
[9] http://ebookarchitects.com/learn-about-ebooks/anatomy-of-an-ebook/

Fixed books can be zoomed as if zooming into a picture. But the text will not reflow, and you will have to pan around to see the page, except on an iBooks app, which will scale the image to best fit the device. The fixed books are primarily images with text overlays. Every word of text must be typed into the file.

Because an FXL file is a single file for every page and is programmed to "fix" the position of every object on the page, it requires extra labor and is often two to three times more expensive to create. The "fixed" layout in Adobe Dreamweaver uses pixels as its unit of measure for specifying the width of your content.

The benefit of fixed format is that the EPUB2 formatting within the file allows the designer to adjust the location of some design elements on the page, giving far greater control over how the page is laid out. Thus a fixed layout book has the advantage of looking more nearly like its companion printed book.

The disadvantage is that, unless programmed otherwise, it will look the same no matter what the size of a device's display screen. On some screens, you may need to scroll left or right, up or down to see everything on the page. Only a few devices can handle fixed format books. Currently only Kindle Fire and

Apple devices can read iBooks. To gain a better understanding of fixed layout, see a demonstration on the SiteWizard.com[10]

Relative Layout

A **relative layout** in web design is one that uses a "relative" unit of measurement (usually a percentage) to specify the width of the page. The content of the page resizes to adapt to the size of the browser window on the device display.

The page layout stretches or shrinks to fill the browser window according to its size. This type of layout can also be called liquid, fluid, elastic or flexible since the page spreads to fill the width of a browser window the way liquid spreads onto a surface.

Print-on-demand

Print-on-demand (POD) is a digital printing method that allows for short runs of printed books — from one copy to a hundred or more. POD is a great tool for testing a book title to see if it has a market. You can print a few POD books as you sell them, rather than using a large offset press run that usually requires a minimum order of 1,000 to 5,000 or more. A large run can mildew in your garage, if the title isn't as successful as you

---

[10] https://www.fbdemo.com/fixed/index.html

hope, and you can also go to offset if the book takes off well. In recent years, the quality of POD books has vastly improved, enabling the format to become more widely acceptable in the marketplace.

As in the case of e-book production, a manuscript submitted to a POD printer must follow certain guidelines. Most POD printers prefer that you submit the book in Adobe PDF format, with individual settings required (such as all fonts embedded in the file). The work must be in its final form. POD printers usually do not provide editorial services and insist that absolutely no editorial changes be made after submission.

The leader in print-on-demand is Lightning Source, a division of Ingram Content Group. Most other entities claiming to be POD printers are third-party agents without printing presses of their own. They use Lightning Source to print the product and skim a little money for themselves in the process. The practice holds true even for Create Space, Amazon's print arm. Lightning Source has a proprietary template which you can use as a guide for setting up an error-free POD title.

Tip: We highly recommend that you not attempt to use the same POD file as your source file for the e-book version. They require two different sets of specifications.

Generally, printers require you to send the designed book to them in a specific PDF format. You can download and use the detailed templates provided by either Lightning Source or Create Space to accurately lay out your cover, book interior, and spine. Both LightningSource.com[11] and Amazon's Create Space[12] offer detailed instructions and templates for creating your POD book. You can also hire a POD book designer to do the job.

LightningSource.com expects to receive a print-ready manuscript and cover files and will not perform editorial work such as proofreading, editing for content, typesetting or making font alterations throughout a book. A digital file must be "print ready" and sent by the digital file submission instructions. A print-ready file ensures that no problems are encountered during the manufacturing process. Files are processed as received and are not pre-flighted (that is to say, quality checked) before processing.

Print-on-demand printers do not make any editing or image manipulations to your file without charging you a hefty fee. And often they won't touch a color book, period. So be sure you have your PDF file set up correctly before you submit. Author

---

[11] http://www.lightningsource.com/
[12] https://www.createspace.com/

Ryan McSwain[13] has a great starter tutorial on pre-flight requirements on his website, and many other tutorials abound on the web. Do read all the vendor's guidelines before you submit.

Tip: *The latest all-in-one service for authors is IngramSpark,*
which offers both E-Book distribution and print-on-demand
printing. We will talk more about these services later.

File Size Matters

Large files can cause unusual production headaches for you and the retailer. Be aware of the size of your manuscript file (usually a PDF or Word Doc file).

Restrictions May Apply

Some retailers restrict the size of a file based on the type of publisher account you have. If you exceed these specifications, the file may not convert into the sales channel at all. Amazon Kindle Digital Platform (KDP), for example, allows files up to 650

---

[13] https://ryanmcswain.wordpress.com/2015/09/22/one-easy-trick-to-improve-your-print-on-demand-book/

MB in Word Doc, Docx, PDF, MOBI, EPUB or HTML. KDP also limits image size to 5 MB.

Font sizes and styles, paragraph spacing and especially images all quickly bloat the size of your file.

What's a Byte?

The website, What's a Byte[14], has a good definition of file sizes.

They define **Megabyte** this way: "A Megabyte is approximately 1,000 Kilobytes. In the early days of computing, a Megabyte was considered to be a large amount of data. These days with a 500 **Gigabyte** hard drive on a computer being common, a Megabyte doesn't seem like much anymore. One of those old 3-1/2 inch floppy disks can hold 1.44 Megabytes or the equivalent of a small book. One hundred Megabytes (100) might hold a couple of volumes of Encyclopedia. Six hundred (600) Megabytes is about the amount of data that will fit on a CD-ROM disk." A **kilobyte** equals about two or three paragraphs of plain text. A megabyte equals about four 200-pages books of plain text. You can see the size of a **Word Docx** file by looking at the file in your file folders while in FILES/VIEW/DETAILS, in the right-most column. It looks something like this:

---

[14] http://www.whatsabyte.com/

Unlocking-secrets-...   5/1/2016 1:08 PM   Microsoft Word D...   1,070 KB

Figure 3. File Size View

In the example above, the file, as it looked in development without pictures, is just over 1,000 Kilobytes.

Larger Files Can Impact Profits

Also, retailers such as Amazon charge a premium on every sale, if your file exceeds a certain size. Amazon calls this extra fee "delivery costs."

Under Amazon's 70% royalty plan, the retailer adds delivery fees to the cost of every unit sold, and charges vary by file size and territory. They are equal to the number of megabytes Amazon determines your Digital Book file contains, multiplied by the Delivery Cost rate of each country in which you distribute. In the US the rate is $0.15/MB listed below, which can eat into your slim profits in a hurry.

Tip: Delivery fees do not apply if you choose the 35% royalty plan.

PART I

CHAPTER 1

How E-Book and Print-on-Demand Distribution Methods Work

Types of Distributors

How many distributors do you need? The answer is: as many as possible! Distribution is a numbers game. The more sales outlets you have, the greater the chance of making a sale. In the old days, when Barnes & Noble had 3,000 stores or more, all you needed to do to make a fair living selling your book was to sell one single book a month in each of those outlets. The logic still applies, though the terrain has become more treacherous with competition.

You don't necessarily need to hire a third party distributor to have your book displayed for sale at retail outlets or catalogs. You can set up your publishing accounts with all the major retailers — including Amazon, Barnes & Noble, Apple iBooks and Kobo — using author portals. The do-it-yourself approach has several advantages. This strategy saves you money and gives you greater control.

There are four main types of distributors you can use to self-distribute your work. The lines between these types can sometimes overlap.

1. **Digital distributor/fulfillment house/wholesaler** usually has an exclusive contract with the publisher (in this case, you) to sell to other wholesalers and retailers actively

2. **Aggregators** are third-party middlemen who take an extra big cut out of your royalties. Some examples are Smashwords and Book Baby.

3. **Direct store programs/self-serve portals** work as the new kind of distributor, which endeavors to eliminate the traditional fulfillment house.

4. **Subscription web sites/outlets**, offering their subscribers access to your book, often for the purpose of pooling earnings and divvying them up among participating authors.

5. **Traditional distributors** A dying or changing species

All of these methods take a chunk out of the retail price of your book, some more than others. The most challenging aspect of self-distribution is to understand the difference between exclusive and non-exclusive agreements and how choosing a distribution method can impact your income. First, let's do some ground work.

Digital Distributor VS Wholesaler: What Is the Difference?

If you simply want to hand over all the intricacies of account setup, distribution, sales tracking and accounting to someone else, perhaps a **distributor** or **wholesaler** is the best choice for you. There is a distinct difference between the two.

The **distributor** works directly with you, the publisher, to sell to various retail and wholesale outlets. You are that company's client. The distributor usually has an active sales force — in some cases, boots on the ground calling on retail stores that represent you and your titles. They handle all order fulfillment, credit, and collections and often carry an inventory of your printed books in stock. To reach the numerous wholesalers out there in the wide world, the publisher must work exclusively through the distributor. Direct association between the publisher and retailers isn't permitted.

The **wholesaler**, on the other hand, will sell your book on a non-exclusive basis. The wholesaler sells directly to other wholesalers/retailers. You supply the product that the wholesaler sells to its clients. They handle all order fulfillment, credit, and collections; and may stock printed books. The wholesaler technically doesn't work for you. The company works for itself on behalf of its customers, who are retailers and other wholesalers. Ingram Content Group is an example of a wholesale distributor that also now offers an author portal for smaller publishers via its IngramSpark service.

So, the distributor works for you directly, and the wholesale works for itself, fulfilling orders for its retail clients.

Understanding the Traditional Wholesale Pricing Model

The traditional method for pricing of a book is known as the "**wholesale pricing model**." Understanding how the system works will help you discern how changes in the underlying structure, such as lower book prices and subscription models can affect your earnings.

There are many wholesalers, both large and regional, with Ingram being the largest. For the wholesaler to be able to give the retailer the 40% discount a store needs to re-sell the book, the wholesaler has to receive a higher discount, often 55%, from you or the distributor. If the wholesaler obtains the book through a distributor, the distributor gets a 15% cut (55%-15%). Wholesalers are aggregators. They do not market make the books they carry; they simply make them available for purchase. Here is how the wholesale pricing model works:

- Retail price of the book: $12.99
- Distributor signs an exclusive contract to sell your book.
- Distributor sells the book to a wholesaler for $5.84 (55% off retail price)
- Distributor keeps 15% ($1.94) of retail price out of the wholesaler's $5.84 earnings
- Wholesaler retains $3.90
- Wholesaler sells the book to a retailer at 40% off. Retailer pays: $7.80
- Retailer sells the book to you for $12.99
- Retailer earns: $5.19 (before royalties and fees)
- You earn about $2 to $3.00 per sale, depending on the royalty plan you have chosen, whether the retailer figures your royalty on the net or gross amount of the sale, and any other fees deducted.

Keep in mind that using either of these likely will require you to have your book already in typeset form in a format acceptable to e-book distribution.

TRADITIONAL DISTRIBUTOR VS WHOLESALER

Distributor

- Exclusive agreement—has active sales force
- Handles all order fulfillment, credit, and collections; stocks printed books
- Publisher goes through distributor to sell to all wholesalers and retailers
- Works at the publisher level.

Wholesaler

- Nonexclusive agreement—directly sells to other wholesalers/retailers
- Handles all order fulfillment, credit, and collections; may stock printed books
- Works on the customer level.

Figure 4. Distributor V Wholesaler, at a glance

What Is an Aggregator?

The **aggregator** produces e-book and print content and has contracted with various partner networks to distribute via a network of partner outlets. They are third-party middlemen between you and various sales outlets. They usually want an exclusive contract with you, meaning they are the only ones who can sell your book. Examples of big aggregators are Smashwords and Book Baby. We will have more to say about these services later in the book.

If you choose to work with an aggregator, expect to pay handsomely for the convenience, and it will likely be harder for you to track sales on a timely basis because the aggregator becomes another layer of management between you and the retailer who sells your book. You, the publisher, are the aggregator's client, but they really work for themselves. They make their real money from charging you for pre-production tasks, such as cover design, interior layout — the necessary steps that come before actual conversion to an e-book format, as well as the conversion (think programming) itself. Even some retailers, such as Barnes & Noble Nook, have also begun offering book design.

Usually, the aggregator will take your raw manuscript and turn it into an e-book format for you. But chances are, you won't be able to take that file elsewhere if you decide you want to leave.

What Is an Author Portal?

An **author portal** is an online account with a major retailer specifically designed for the small publisher or independent author. Portals offer the author or small press the ability to directly monitor and manage their distribution without the use of third-party management companies for production and distribution which can eat into the author's already-slim profit margins.

The Portal Process: After you establish your account and ID and password, you can use a retailer's **author portal** to upload and sell your book, manage your content and sales reports through your retail account.

You must transform your manuscript from a word processing program or other software into an acceptable e-book format, such as EPUB or Mobi for Kindle. Simple books with mostly text and limited graphics may be uploaded directly to a conversion tool residing on the retailer's website. However, more complex books may require you to hire a professional conversion house to turn your raw manuscript (usually an MS Word document or PDF) to the necessary digital files.

Once you have an EPUB or Mobi file in hand, you can then upload the finished file into your retail account and post the book for sale on the retailer's site.

The alternative to the direct author-to-retailer portal is a hybrid production and distribution company that manages both functions but most likely utilizes the same outlets you would use if using the direct retail portals.

What Is Metadata
and Why Is It Necessary?

Think of **metadata** as your book description. Before you begin to upload your files, you will want to assemble all the metadata required for your book. The descriptions include the book title, subtitle, author(s), brief description, ISBN (International Standard Book Number), price, book category (i.e. romance, mystery, nonfiction) and territories in which you want to sell the book.

All of these bits of information go together to identify your book — the metadata. Today, this information must be structured to be read across many different computers, devices, and platforms. The way you now enter a book description into a retailer's catalog isn't always as simple as typing in some regular text, though it may appear that way to the casual user. Part of this metadata description involves machine-readable subject or category headings.

The publishing industry has established certain standard ways to identify and categorize books based on topical content. The **BISAC Subject Headings List**, also known as the BISAC Subject Codes List, has become an industry-wide standard. In fact, without the proper subject code for your book, many booksellers and libraries may not be able to load your title into their system for customer discovery or download.

BISAC is an acronym for Book Industry Standards and Communications. The Book Industry Study Group oversees the system. The Subject Heading applied to a book can determine where to shelve a work in a brick and mortar store or define how the book will be searched within an internal database. Thus, it is vital in helping readers find your book.

When you are inputting metadata into your various retail accounts, you may be asked to enter the subject category as a specific programming code.

Instead of simply typing "general fiction" or "action/adventure fiction" in the subject/ category field, you will need to look up and enter the specific BISAC code for that category. For example, you will enter the general fiction category on the retailer's form like this, with a machine-readable number as part of the description:

> FIC000000 FICTION / General
> FIC002000 FICTION / Action & Adventure

Tip: *A complete list of BISAC codes can be found here on the Book Industry Study Group site.*[15]

All of your other data, including pricing and sales territories, must also be entered in a certain "structured" way. Each bit of information that describes the book now must be precisely input.

---

[15] https://www.bisg.org/bisac/complete-bisac-subject-headings-2015-edition

To enter your book information, you can simply use the specific retailer's metadata form or template (usually a preformatted spreadsheet). Sometimes the form is built into the retailer's upload process, so all you will see is simple text headers for each field instead of programming code.

If you are doing several titles at a time, however, it may be more beneficial to request an official metadata spreadsheet from the retailer and send them one finished form containing all titles. These forms look like sophisticated pre-formed spreadsheets with the fields labeled and encoded in industry-accepted structure.

Some vendors may ask you (especially if you have multiple titles) to send the book data using an **ONIX**-compliant management system — one that has been developed by a third-party software company. It is a good idea to have some notion of what they mean.

The **ONIX for Books Product Information Message** is *the* international standard for representing and communicating book industry product information in electronic form. It's important to understand that ONIX is simply a standardized specification for communicating book information. It is not in itself a database, a software application, or a product or service that you can purchase. Although many software applications and databases may well implement the ONIX standard, most major book retailers use this underlying architecture to create their metadata forms and templates. The actual ONIX specification and associated documents are available and usable without charge at the non-profit organization, Editeur. Full membership requires a fee. EDItEUR is the international development coordinator for the standards infrastructure of electronic commerce in the book and e-book industry.

If you don't want to develop your metadata system to comply with ONIX standards, many **EDItEUR** members and other organizations provide commercial off-the-shelf software or web-based applications for product management that implement ONIX messaging into your publisher's retail account. Remember, many accounts won't load a book into their system unless a BISAC is assigned.

Tip: For those who want an in-depth look at the messaging downloads of the latest ONIX and instructions you can find them here. [16]

---

[16] http://www.editeur.org/93/Release-3.0-Downloads/

Manual Metadata Template

If you don't have ONIX or a special web app and you have
multiple titles to upload, the retailer may send you a simple
metadata spreadsheet to complete. The form will be designed to
comply with ONIX formatting, but you can open it in standard
Excel software, fill in the fields and submit the completed
document to the retailer. Some content fields will be required
and others are optional as shown below.

Required Metadata Information	Reference ID for the title. Using the eISBN is highly recommended
	Imprint
	Book title
	Author(s)
Optional Metadata Information	Print book ISBN
	eISBN If no eISBN is available use an alternate alphanumeric identifier

Figure 5. Metadata requirements

Online Metadata Input Screen
for a Single Title

Here's an example of a retailer's *online* metadata form, in this
case for Kindle. When you have a publishing account with
Amazon and you are logged in, you can edit the **Metadata** for

each title you have uploaded into your KDP library. It looks
something like this.

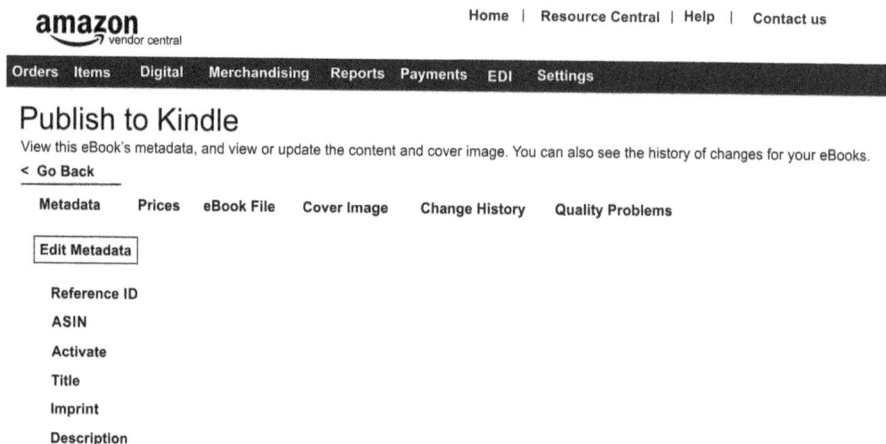

Figure 6. KDP Metadata Example

You will get paid certain royalties from each sale the site makes
for you and you will have instant access to the retailer's sales
reports through your account "dashboard." A dashboard is a
central set of online tools that reside on the retailer's site. They
let you add, edit and delete content and images, add
descriptions, set pricing, select territories or countries which you
wish to make your title available.

You can quickly see what you are earning, but be aware that
sales reports in your author account usually lag by three months
or more from the time of a sale, because invoicing and customer
payment require processing through the multiple channels

involved in selling your book. All in all, however, the author portal is the most direct line between you and the reading buyer.

Some author portals offer exclusive royalty plans; some do not and a few offer both options. Amazon, for example, lets you choose between a 35% and 70% royalty rate if you know where they have hidden the 35% plan. They'd rather coerce you into the 70% plan which makes them the exclusive seller of your work. While a 70% deal looks better than the other one at first glance, it may turn out to be a dark pit, if your distribution strategy isn't right. We will explain some of the hidden traps in royalty rates in later chapters and the advantages and disadvantages of signing an exclusive contract vs maintaining non-exclusive status.

The best-known retailers who offer author portals are:

- Amazon Kindle
- Apple iBooks
- Barnes & Noble Nook
- Kobo Books

You can optimize your audience exposure (called "reach") by carefully developing a strategy that includes all of these, rather than just one or two.

What Is The Subscription Model?

The **Subscription Model** is the latest scheme for online retailers to boost their profits. They offer the content you worked so hard to produce to a large pool of visitors who pay the service a monthly or annual fee. In return for that fee, subscribers get access to all the content for sale in the site's online catalog. Meanwhile, the author gets paid when a subscriber reads beyond a certain portion of a book. If the reader reads a little bit of the book, the author gets nothing. If the reader reads most of the book, the author gets paid.

But authors do not earn the full retail price of the book — like what they would have received on a straight sale.

All the books that qualify as having been read that month, for example, go into a pool and royalties are divvied up among the lucky ones — much like a tips pool for waiters or a lottery. Meanwhile, the subscription site rakes in monthly subscription fees, regardless of who reads what.

Amazon Select, in which Amazon Prime subscribers get full access to any and all books they'd like, is the biggest purveyor of the Subscription Model. Another large subscription site is Scribd. Scribd doesn't accept content directly under its subscription model. Authors must go through Smashwords to have their book products listed. Scribd also does have a direct program.

More about these programs later.

Traditional Distributors

The **traditional distributor** mostly handled long print runs of the soft cover and printed books, warehousing large in-stock quantities for sale to retailers such as Barnes & Noble Bookstores. They represent the publisher on an exclusive basis via an active sales force and handle all aspects of distribution. But many now handle e-books and print-on-demand titles as well. It is harder these days to tell the difference between a traditional distributor and a new one.

Ingram Content Group serves publishers in the traditional sense but also owns Lightning Source, a print-on-demand production facility serving smaller publishers and authors, and IngramSpark, a new author portal.

Among others are Baker & Taylor, focusing on libraries; Independent Publishers Group (IPG), owned by Chicago Review Press; Midpoint Trade Books, Inc., for independent publishers and Small Press Distribution (SPD) a non-profit literary arts distributor.

TIP: *Here's a list of Independent Book Distributors:*
http://www.bookmarket.com/distributors.htm

Not All Publisher Accounts
Are Created Equal

The industry once clearly segmented some publishers from others, giving a select group the best wholesale discount rates, better in-store displays, and other perks. Bookstores gave self-published authors the cold shoulder. Major distribution firms largely ignored smaller presses altogether. Only consortiums such as Perseus Books Group, an independent company committed to independent publishers, would handle the little guys.

Since the 1990's when technology made it easier and cheaper for authors to self-publish without much outside help, the practice has wildly grown to overshadow traditional publishing by a big house. **Vanity publishers** who charged authors huge sums of money to produce and distribute their books have also declined. But self-publishers often still do not command the same publishing terms and can't always access the same tools available to large publishers — even in today's world.

Having a "publisher" account on an author portal doesn't mean you have the same standing as a larger publisher.

While the Internet has blurred the line between the big guys and the rest of us, there remains a large difference between the two ways of doing business. Discrimination still exists to some degree, despite Amazon's apparent anything-goes philosophy. The tactics are just more subtle, Amazon included.

Larger publishing houses have access to more sophisticated systems than those provided to the self-published author. Often these advanced sites offer broader support for different file types, streamlined systems for accepting or ingesting titles and different rules for discount rates and pricing.

Aggregators, self-distribution portals and subscription sites, all cater to the small publisher or author who has from ten to 100 titles or so per year.

Corporate Philosophy

How retailers treat small publishers varies based on corporate attitudes, business philosophy, goals, and level of greed.

Strategically, Ingram, the largest book distributor in the world, has done more than about any other distributor to design programs that fit both large and small publishers. Ingram Content serves the big guys, and IngramSpark satisfies the needs of smaller ones, perhaps better than any service out there.

It appears that Amazon Kindle's strategy is to knock out the large publishers all together and become "the" publisher for anyone who writes a book. Period. Their goal, it seems, is to own all content. In 2016 the giant retailer began opening brick-and-mortar book stores in several cities with a plan to open some 400 physical outlets, according to GeekWire.com.

Apple iBooks looks to be striving to treat all publishers equally, as does Kobo Books, based in Canada and now owned by a Japanese company, Rakuten, one of the world's largest online retail marketplaces.

In every case, some differences between big and small publisher accounts do exist.

If you are unaware of the differences from the start, you may be thwarted by certain key restrictions after you've gone to a lot of trouble and money to produce your product.

Many constraints are related to what current technology can and cannot handle in an e-book file and on the capabilities of the retailer's software systems used to recognize and handle the codes that underlie your e-book file. These are the most important restrictions to look for:

- **Pricing**: What you can charge for your book in some cases is limited by the size of your file, whether you have a print version. Apple's iTunes (for iBooks store) restricts pricing based on your file size.

- **File size:** A retailer may reject your book, if you do not know the limits for each outlet you plan to include in your distribution plan. For example, Barnes & Noble Nook limits the size of files for its publisher portal to 20 MB. IngramSpark limits file size to 100 MB, while large publishers with traditional publisher accounts are not subjected to the same limits. Apple iTunes allows a maximum file size of 2 GB. In later chapters, we present brief profiles of each major vendor related to audience reach, royalty rates, and some key restrictions.

- **Graphics**: Some retailers restrict the number of graphics or images they can handle in an e-book file. If you have a book that contains main images, go to each retailer's author portal and search for photo, image or graphics restrictions. Also be aware that graphs, equations, and maps do not translate well to the simple e-book, which may require special formatting. Even if you have specialized formatting, know that the file may be readable only by a few devices, such as Kindle Fire and ioS devices like Apple iPad and iPhone.

- **Format:** Most people are aware that Amazon has its proprietary e-book format, called Mobi. While Amazon does accept EPUB files on its author/publisher portal, books in this format potentially can deliver a poor reader experience, unless the book has a very basic design. Mobi or fixed-format files are the best choices for more involved designs.

Challenges
of Do-It-Yourself Distribution

Devising a distribution plan that maximizes your visibility in the crowded marketplace first requires you to define your target audience and establish an overall goal.

- Beyond major markets, are there secondary markets you might explore?
- What audiences might find your book appealing? Young? Old? What are their interests?
- At what price are similar books selling for in your category?
- What geographical territories should you consider, the US only? Canada? Europe?
- Which retailers are likely to reach your target audience?
- How can you avoid conflict (duplication) in multiple sales channels? As we mentioned earlier, conflict in distribution channels occurs when you submit the same title to several vendors who then, in turn, feed your title to the same sales

outlet. Such a mistake could cause a retailer to pull your title from a sales catalogue. You will need to understand what each retailer offers in the way of "opt out" clauses to avoid this sort of duplication. For example, IngramSpark lets you opt out of Kindle distribution if you already have an Amazon Kindle publishing agreement in place. Ingram feeds Amazon content. So, the "opt out" provision keeps the title from being duplicated in the same retail catalogue. Be sure to read the fine print, especially if you are considering an aggregator. Some aggregators and distributors can't distribute your title at all if you have already listed the work in another sales channel. Researching the market with these questions in mind is imperative to your success.

Here are a few questions to ask yourself when devising your distribution strategy:

- How do retailers' pricing rules impact your income?
- How might signing an exclusive deal work against you?
- If using retailer's built-in content creation tools, how might they restrict you in using the finished file in other markets?
- How might unclear fees eat into your royalty earnings?

- What tricks do retailers use to make royalty rates look better than they are?

CHAPTER 2

How Royalty Plans Impact Your Earnings

It is important that you clearly understand how retailers calculate royalties. What may seem like a great deal could, in fact, cost you more earnings in the long run. Here are some basic definitions.

List Price: The advertised full retail price of the book.

Net price: The publisher's income AFTER the retailer has taken its cut. Additional fees may be deducted from the net price, such as printing costs.

Wholesale discount rate: The discounted rate (price off) at which a publisher offers a book to the retailer is usually 55%. That's not the percentage of the sale you get to keep. It is the percentage you are giving to the retailer off the list price.

Whether the retailer bases the royalty rate on the list price of a book or the net price makes a huge difference in what you earn. Believe it or not, a 70% royalty rate may not earn you as much as a 35% royalty rate depending on whether the retailer calculates the royalty at the net price of the book or the gross price. Be aware as you evaluate individual retailers. Some examples will help you see how this works.

Assume a book sale price of $9.99 and wholesale discount @ 55%:

Vendor A (Smashwords) pays 70% of net = $3.15
Vendor B (Amazon 35% plan) pays 35% of list/gross= $3.50

Where are you likely to make more money and sell more books?

QUICK NET/GROSS EXAMPLE

Assume a book sale price of $9.99 and wholesale discount @ 55%

Vendor A (Smashwords) pays 70% of net = $3.15
Vendor B (Amazon 35% plan) pays 35% of list/gross = $3.50
Where are you likely to make more money and sell more books?

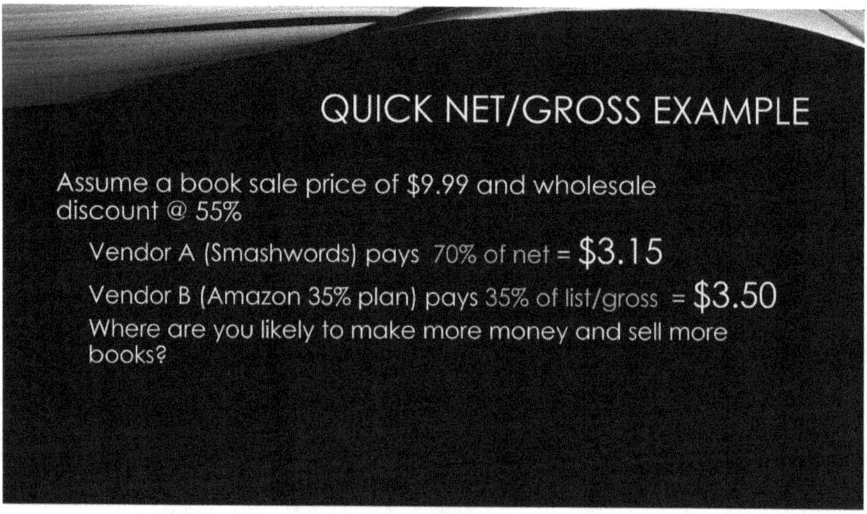

Figure 7. Calculating net and gross

Tip: *Bear in mind that these profit figures do not include the cost of designing, editing and producing the book itself, which we are not covering in this book. We encourage you to thoroughly research before trying to figure out your break-even point (how many books you need to sell at your designated profit margin to cover production costs). Only with these costs included can you determine your real profitability.*

In newer subscription models, your book goes into a pool, and you get paid by how many pages (or sometimes a percentage) of the book are read, as a "share" of all the book pages read that month. As we shall see later, this may not be the best royalty plan for authors.

CHAPTER 3

A Look At The Big Five
Retailer Publishing Portals

Setting Up Your Account

To self-distribute to the four biggest retailers, you need only set up your publisher/author account on the website or portal for each one. Chapter 3 includes links to the major retailers' sign up pages. The first step will be to establish an ID and password on the site and fill out legal and banking information. Typically a retailer will have a "dashboard" where you can upload your book and manage content and sales reports. You do not have to use their built-in production tools. Third-party production and conversion houses offer higher quality and more flexibility. They can also solve content problems faster and more efficiently. That saves you from battling through retailers' help forums.

One of the most difficult concepts to grasp is that of duplicated or conflicting sales channels. Again, a conflict occurs when one retail service feeds the same retail sales outlets the same information as does another. So, the receiving store is getting the same identical book from two different sources, often under different stock or ISBN numbers. Such conflict causes havoc with the retailers' systems of ingesting and indexing files. The only way to avoid the problem is to offer the author a choice of feeds he/she wants to use to display the title in a particular sales channel. For example, IngramSpark feeds Amazon Kindle titles. If you already have an account set up with Kindle, then if Ingram also supplies that title for sale to Kindle you have a conflict. Retailers should offer you the option to "opt out" of one feed or the other to avoid the problem. Not all retailers feed one another, making duplication a non-issue. Kobo, for example, doesn't feed Amazon title information, so they don't care whether you are simultaneously selling the book on Amazon Kindle. You don't have to worry, because the retailer will tell you its restrictions. It is a good idea to be aware of the issue and any potential conflicts that could arise from your planning strategy.

Here we have capsuled information about each site's eligibility, exclusivity, "reach" (how many retail outlets and territories they distribute to), duplication policies, their royalty rates and key restrictions, quirks and live links to their sign-up pages.

1. IBOOKS STORE VIA ITUNES CONNECT[17]

- **Eligibility:** Accepts most anybody of legal age. (You must sign an e-book distribution agreement)
- **Exclusive?** No, unless you created the work with iBooks Author tool
- **Reach:** 51 territories worldwide
- **Royalty Rate:** 70% of list price
- **Key Restrictions:**
    - E-book without a companion print edition: You can set any "reasonable" price (Apple may reject).
    - E-book with companion print edition priced at ± $22: Maximum e-book price is $9.99 for first 12 months.
    - E-book with bestseller print edition priced at $9.99 to $40: E-book price must be from $9.99 to $19.99.
- **File Size:** Keep the following points in mind about the file size of your book:

    1. The maximum file size is 2 GB.

---

[17] http://www.apple.com/itunes/working-itunes/sell-content/books/

2. The larger the file size, the longer it takes for a book to download to the user's device.

3. To optimize download time, keep your book file under 1 GB.

4. Customers using 4G or other cellular networks cannot download books or book samples larger than 100 MB and must instead connect to Wi-Fi to download.

Tip: *Check the size of an EPUB file using Finder OS X on a Mac computer or Explorer in Windows. You can also check the approximate file size of a book created with iBooks Author (if you are working in an Apple environment) by using the program's Document Inspector to tell you the file size including all the graphics or charts used in the book.*

---

2. AMAZON KINDLE DIRECT PUBLISHING (KDP)[18]

- **Eligibility:** Accepts most anyone of legal age
- **Exclusive?** Depends on the plan you pick. They push an exclusive contract. Be careful not to opt in unknowingly. See critical details in Chapter 5
- **Reach:** Who knows? Their unverified market share = 60% or more
- **Duplication:** The exclusive plan does not allow any overlap or conflict with other channels. If you use multiple retail channels, and you already have a listing with Amazon Kindle, you will need to "opt out" of the other channels that also district to Kindle.
- **Royalty Rates (3 options):**
  - 35% nonexclusive
  - 70% exclusive (without Amazon Select)

---

[18] https://kdp.amazon.com/

- 70% exclusive with Amazon Select plan

This plan automatically places your book in Kindle Unlimited (KU) and the Kindle Owners Lending Library (KOLL). This plan gives "Amazon Prime" subscribers free access to your entire work. The author's pay is based on the number of pages read via a shared author royalty "pool." The plan requires you to give absolute exclusivity to Amazon. See Chapter 5 for more critical details BEFORE you sign up. If you click one tiny box in the sign-up process, you will wind up in Amazon Select, whether you intended to do so or not. We do NOT recommend this subscription plan. So be careful not to click the box if you want to avoid this automatic trap.

Kindle Income Example:

Assume a sale price of $9.99 (excluding delivery costs, fees, and VAT taxes):

- Income at 35% of list: $3.49
- Income at 70% of list (non-Select plan): $6.99

Note: You will lose 30-40% of the market on the 70% plan. See Chapter 5 for royalty effect in Amazon Select.

KDP INCOME EXAMPLE

Assume a sale price of $9.99 (excluding delivery costs, fees, and VAT taxes):
- Income at 35% of list: $3.49
- Income at 70% of list: $6.99
  - But you will lose 30–40% of any additional market with an exclusive contract.

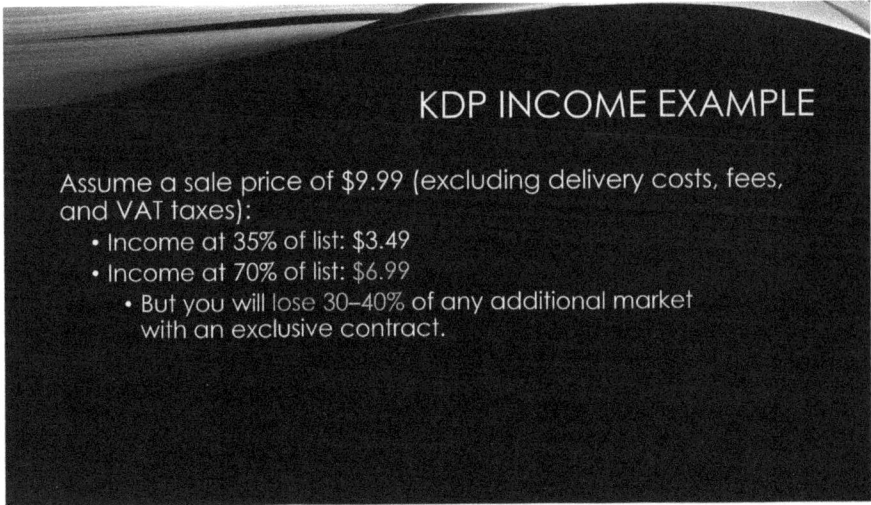

Figure 8. Income example

- **Key Restrictions:**

  - **Exclusive!** If you sign an exclusive plan with Kindle, you will lose the opportunity to sell your books in any additional market.

- **Price:** Minimum and maximum price restrictions apply to all plans, based on file size.

KDP 35% PLAN: PRICE LIMITED BASED ON FILE SIZE	
$0.99-$200	File size = less than 3 mb
$1.99-$200	File size = 3 to 10 mb
$2.99-$200	File size = greater than 10 mb

Figure 9. KDP file size limits

- **Delivery Fees:** In the 70% royalty plan you may be charged a "delivery fee" based on the size (number of megabytes) in your file. In the U.S., the delivery cost is about 15 cents per megabyte, which can significantly eat into your profit margin. The delivery fee does not apply if you choose the 35% royalty plan.

- **Other Potential Catches**

  - The 70% royalty deal automatically renews every 90 days, meaning the plan continues until you yell stop and go through the notification process.

  - After you cancel or withdraw, you must wait 90 days before selling anywhere else. The waiting period applies every time your account automatically renews.

- If you have a print book in any other channel, the e-book must be priced at least 20% below the print book.
- **Examples:**

If a print book sells at $9.99, the e-book must sell for $7.99 or less. As another example: if you have a print book selling for $29.95, the most you can sell the e-book for would be $10.99, so it is probably best to price the e-book at the most attractive price point, which is $9.99.

Biggest Catch of All

Amazon Select author royalty pool lets Amazon Prime subscribers read your book for free. The plan lacks real income potential unless you hit their bestseller or featured list. More about this in later chapters.

3. NOOK PRESS BY BARNES & NOBLE[19]

- **Eligibility:** Adults. Vendor agreement required.
- **Exclusive?** No
- **Reach:** Eight countries, including the US, and Europe, via BN.com and various apps.
- **Duplication:** There are few conflicts due to unique devices and apps. Nook doesn't distribute e-books to iBooks and Kindle.
- **Royalty Rate based on list price:**

  - 65% on books priced at $2.99–$9.99
  - 40% on books above or below these price points

  Effect of Pricing on Your Income at Nook:
  - Book price of $9.99:
    - Royalty @ 65%: You earn $6.49
  - Book price of $10.99:
    - Royalty @ 40%: You earn $4.39

---

[19] https://www.nookpress.com/

EFFECT OF PRICING ON YOUR INCOME AT NOOK

- Book price of $9.99:
  - Royalty @ 65%: $6.49
- Book price of $10.99:
  - Royalty @ 40%: $4.39

Tip: forget the extra dollar, sell at the lower price!

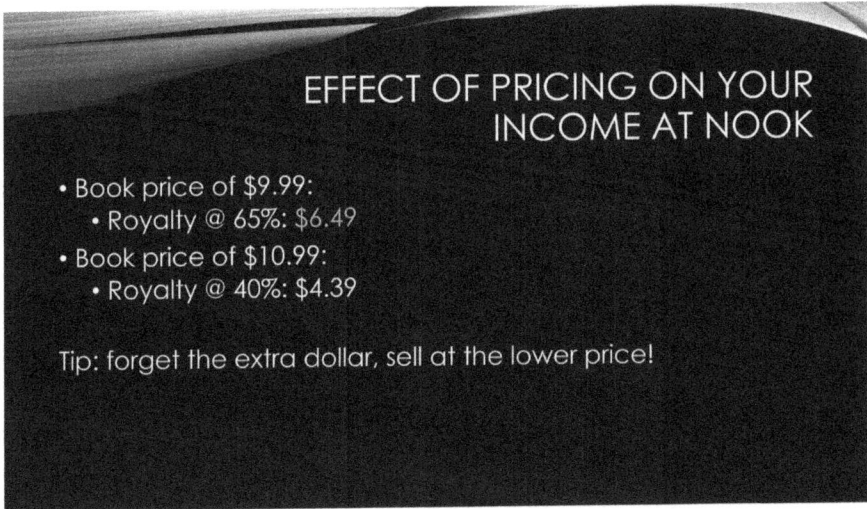

Figure 10. Pricing at Nook

TIP: Forget the extra dollar you would make on the book at $10.99. The royalty you earn will be less for the 65% plan and keep your book priced at $9.99 or less.

- **Key Restrictions:**

  - File size limit: 20 MB (Nook Press)

Important Note: NOOK no longer sells digital content in the United Kingdom, as Barnes & Noble continues to try to stem recent losses (effective in early 2016). The NOOK Store on NOOK devices sold in the UK, on the UK NOOK Reading App for Android and at www.nook.com/gb ceased operation. Users continue to have access to the vast majority of books they have already purchased on Nook Books via Sainsbury's Entertainment on Demand[20]. The change does not affect NOOK in the United States. For the third quarter of Fiscal 2016, NOOK sales of $51.7 million decreased 33.3% due primarily to lower device and content sales.

---

[20] https://www.sainsburysentertainment.co.uk/

4. KOBO WRITING LIFE (AUTHOR PORTAL)

Kobo Writing Life[21] is the self-publishing portal for Kobo, based in Canada and owned by Japan's Rakuten, one of the largest online retailers in the world.

- **Eligibility:** Adults
- **Exclusive?** No
- **Reach:** 32 territories, 200 countries. See Page 13 in Kobo's User Guide[22] for details.
- **Royalty Rate:**
  - 70% of suggested retail price (SRP) in the 32 Independent Publishing Program (IPP) territories, ranging from the U.S, Canada, certain Europe countries, and others. For a list of territories where

---

[21] https://www.kobo.com/writinglife?style=onestore&store=US
[22] http://download.kobobooks.com/writinglife/en-US/KWL-User-Guide.pdf

Kobo pays the higher rate, download the User Guide[23] (Page 13)

- 45% outside IPP territories

- **Key Restrictions:**
  1. File size limit: 35 MB
  2. Price restrictions: The price range for which you can sell a book on this portal and earn the 70% royalty rate is between $2.99 and $9.99. Books which sell outside this range earn the lesser royalty rate.
  3. Duplication: Kobo's reading devices, much like Amazon's, are proprietary. Thus a book read on a Kobo device will not be counted as a book read on a Kindle device. The buyer is less apt to buy the same book on two different sales outlets for two different devices, though it is possible. Thus, there isn't much concern over duplication in its sales channels.

- The impact of Territories: Question: Are you selling mostly inside or outside of Canadian territories? Let's do some quick calculations:
  - Inside the Canadian territories you earn: 70% on $9.99 book = $6.99
  - Outside Canadian territories you earn: 45% on $9.99 book = $4.49

---

[23] http://download.kobobooks.com/writinglife/en-US/KWL-User-Guide.pdf

---

TIP: To be sure you earn the most, study page 26 of Kobo's pricing guide[24] for each territory in which you want to distribute. Kobo has a handy tool that lets you enter the pricing for each territory.

TIP: Take the 70% deal in IPP territories. Use other sales channels for outside regions that may pay more than 45%.

KOBO PUBLISHER OPERATIONS[25]

- **Eligibility:** Publishers who have a larger backlist of titles, can apply to Kobo Publisher Operations[26], to be considered for a traditional publishing account.
- **Reach:** Publisher Operations distributes to 200 countries.
- **Kobo Publisher Operations:** Publisher Operations utilizes publisher generated EPUBs and ONIX files uploaded through FTP. **ONIX for Books** is the international standard for representing and communicating book industry product information in electronic form. In other words, it's the system used to describe your book to buyers.

---

[24] http://download.kobobooks.com/writinglife/en-US/KWL-User-Guide.pdf
[25] https://www.kobo.com/kobopublisheroperations
[26] https://www.kobo.com/kobopublisheroperations

Tip: *The difference between the Publisher Operations account and the Writing Life publishing account will be in what file formats and sizes are permissible, the methods used to upload files and in fewer pricing restrictions.*

5. INGRAMSPARK

(PART OF INGRAM CONTENT GROUP)

Ingram Content Group is the world's largest distributor of physical and digital content. In the past, they catered only to larger publishers. Now they have their publishing portal for small presses and authors — IngramSpark. IngramSpark is the only publishing platform that delivers fully integrated print and digital distribution services to the book industry through a single source.

- **Eligibility**: IngramSpark accepts authors with less than 100 titles; CoreSource is for larger publishers of digital and print content.
- **Exclusive?** No! You can opt out of any conflicting (duplicated) channels, such as Kindle.
- **Reach:**
  - 70 emerging online e-book retailers.
  - 39,000 ordering systems of global booksellers, libraries, and online retailers around the world.

- Linked to direct orders from web consumer and major mobile and e-reader devices.
- Duplication: Spark does not allow duplication between it and Kindle. "Opt out" choices are available when you sign contract documents in the sign-up process. If your book has been published on Amazon Kindle anytime during the past 12 months, Ingram can't distribute to Kindle. If you published the book on Apple, you must remove the title from the iBook store before uploading to IngramSpark. Note: Reviews /ratings won't transfer back to iBooks store. Essentially you start over with these features. Even if restricted to these sales channels, your book will still have distribution to the more than 70+ Core Source e-retailers.
- **Royalty Rates:**
  - 40% of list price if Spark plan includes Kindle
  - 45% of list if you exclude Kindle and self-distribute directly to Amazon
- **Example:**

Based on book priced at $9.99:

- If Spark also distributes to Kindle: You earn $3.99.
- If Spark does not distribute to Kindle: You earn $4.45.

TIP: For wider distribution and maximum income, earn $3.49 from direct 35% plan on Kindle; take $4.45 on Spark sales without Kindle. Why? Using both may widen your reach by about 30 to 40%.

- **Special Features**

Ingram Content Group, the parent company for IngramSpark, now enables authors to sell their print and digital books directly to readers via their websites, blogs, and social networks, via their newly-acquired subsidiary, **Aer.io**.

The new feature, launched in late 2015, extends the sales network of anyone with a web presence - whether a publisher, author or bookseller - and will provide the ability to sell content worldwide.

Also, through Aer.io's marketing platform Aer.io Flyer, publishers, authors and booksellers can promote e-books and print books with a direct link to buy while taking advantage of Ingram's global distribution network. An author or small publisher can build a whole online store quickly and easily using the Aer.io tools. They do all the order fulfillment and shipping. You manage your account through a very easy dashboard.

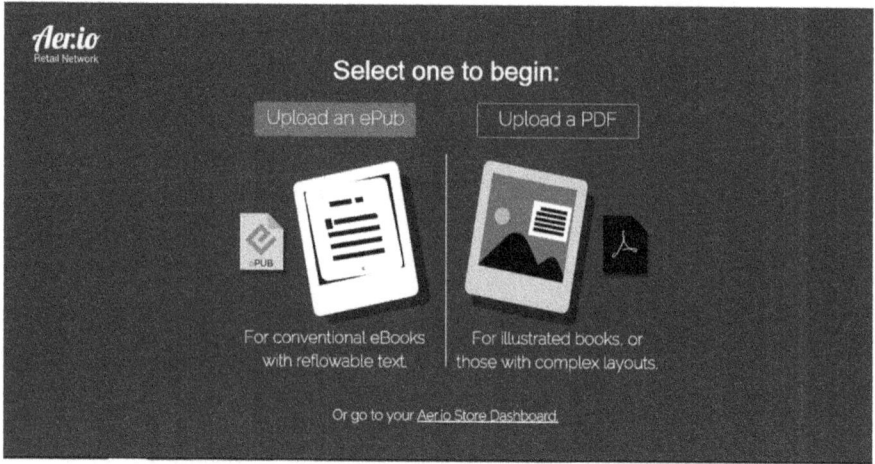

Figure 11. Easy upload interface lets you choose between EPUB and PDF. You can then embed your book or collection into your website or blog.

In addition to Aer.io, IngramSpark has expanded its print capabilities in the UK and Australia with a new program called Global Connect Program (GCP). The move enables Ingram's print-on-demand facility, Lightning Source, to directly provide print and distribution in additional markets, including distribution via Espresso Book Machines at various locations throughout the world. The Espresso Book Machine (EBM) is a print-on-demand (POD) machine that prints, collates, covers, and binds a single book in a few minutes.

Key Preparation Restrictions for E-Books: From IngramSpark EPUB Guide[27]

- **Cover:** For display use on retail partners' websites.

  - **The File must contain front cover only.** Full spread print book jackets that include spine and back cover will be rejected.
  - **Format:** Must be a JPG file
  - **Size:** 2560 pixels on longest side. Minimum 1600 pixels on the shortest side.
  - **Color:** All front covers must be RGB.
  - The content of the cover image must not infringe on another publisher's or artist's copyright on the same cover.

- **Interior:**

  - **Size:** 100MB or less.

  All incoming files must be checked by the International Digital Publishing Forum (IDPF) Validator for accuracy. While IngramSpark and other retail sites can accept

---

[27] https://ingramspark.com/Portal/EPUBGuide

100MB files, when you upload your large file into Spark's system, the Validator cannot check files over 10MB due to the amount of time it would take to process your book. It is possible the validator system will alert you that it has accepted your file when it has not. Thus, you may be sitting there waiting for your book to show up in online retail stores and it never will. If your book file size is more than 10 MB, then it is best to contact a customer service rep to double check if the file was ingested into the sales channel.

- **Format:** EPUB 2 or 3 (flowable text only). Spark cannot accept fixed format or enhanced EPUB files at this time.

  - **Image size:** No single image inside an EPUB can be greater than 3.2 million pixels. (Total pixels = length in pixels x width in pixels).
  - **Include an internal cover image:** This should be formatted in the same size and as part of your interior (for use within the book content).

- **Metadata:** Be sure the metadata entered in IngramSpark matches the information on your cover. For example, if the cover art and the book asset are for a book titled Paradiso, but the metadata is for Purgatorio, then the items do not match.

- **Page Numbers:** There should not be any reference to page numbers in the book. The Table of Contents also should not be numbered (numbers are added by the device on which the book is displayed). Your e-book will never look just like your print book. E-readers are limited in the way they display content, and your book will appear different from device to device.

CHAPTER 4

Big Aggregators

Big aggregators are middlemen who take 10–15% or more of your royalties, above the retailers' cut.

Book Baby[28]

- **Eligibility:** Adults
- **Exclusive?** Yes!
- **Reach:** 60+ stores in 170 countries. Really?
- **Duplication:** You sign an exclusive agreement; you can't distribute to other channels. If your book is displayed on Amazon Kindle Select, Book Baby can't distribute your book to iPad, Nook, Kobo, Kindle, or anywhere else for three months!
- **Fees:** Regular setup fee, $299; cover design up to $279; ISBN, $29; $199 fixed layout; extra charges for additional pages and graphics. May total more than $1,000. An annual fee-based subscription is REQUIRED. How many books must you sell to break even?

---

[28] https://www.bookbaby.com/

- **Example:**
  - Avg. Price of $9.99
    - Avg. net income of $4.50 @ 100% net = 222 books
  - **Royalty Rate (affiliates only):** 100% of the net (less any transaction fees or taxes)
  - **Royalty Rate (Book Baby store only):** 75% of the list price (fewer taxes and fees, chargebacks, non-payment, legal fees)
- **Additional fees:** Book Baby charges 15% on every Book Baby store sale. It is not clear whether this is before or after the 75% royalty.

Smashwords[29]

- **Eligibility:** Adults
- **Exclusive?** No
- **Reach:**
  - Major retailers in 51 countries, including Scribd (subscription service)
- 34,000 libraries and schools via Overdrive[30] libraries
  - Note: Your book must be accepted in Premium Catalogue to qualify. Smashwords only distributes about 200 titles to Amazon. It may be better to go directly to Amazon.
- **Key Restrictions:**
  - If the title exists on Kindle Direct Platform you can also enable Kindle (.mobi) format for Smashwords' store, but it is Digital Rights Management-free (DRM-free), unlike Amazon, which offers DRM. DRM prevents unauthorized redistribution of digital media and restricts the ways consumers can copy content they've purchased.

---

[29] http://wwwsmashwords.com
[30] https://www.overdrive.com/

- **Royalty Rates:**
  - 85% of *net* sales (not the list price) in its store
  - 70% of the net via affiliates (= about 25-30% of the list price). Substantial processing fees of 35 cents or more
  - **Example:** Book sale price of $9.99
    - Less 55% retailer discount -$5.44
    - Net income: $3.15 (at 70% of net)
    - Less transaction fee -.35
    - Author income: $2.79

Pronoun.com[31]
(a different breed of aggregator)

New York-based Vook.com rebranded its website as Pronoun.com, a professional publishing and analytics platform. The author distribution system works differently than most aggregators. While others charge handsome fees for up-front production and conversion, Pronoun.com offers these services free, along with actual distribution at no charge. Authors can convert an edited Word doc to a professionally designed e-book and reach more than 95% of the digital marketplace via Amazon, iBooks, Barnes & Noble, Kobo and Google Play.

We suspect that the conversion tools work well for simple books, but perhaps not for more complex layouts. Also, when something is offered entirely free, one can bet that somewhere, somehow the entity will be either charging fees that aren't readily seen, collecting information for either their own use or sometimes to sell to third parties. (Pronoun.com says it does not share your information with third parties. Interestingly, buried

---

[31] http://www.pronoun.com

deep in their terms is that they have the right to advertise on the screens where your books are displayed and to use your content to promote its services.

Once published on Pronoun.com, you can make unlimited updates to your metadata, track your sales across all five retailers and receive customized suggestions on pricing, positioning and more. All of this is completely free: there are no up-front costs and authors keep 100% of their earnings.

How can Pronoun.com offer such a deal? In addition to offering free services to authors, Pronoun.com also powers the publishing programs of large media companies like *The New York Times*, *Forbes* and *Fast Company*, who are paying partners, along with media outlets, literary agents, brands, consulting firms and other businesses. They don't say much more than that on their site.

The company has investors, including some of the most successful venture capital firms, who are supporting the new publishing model and make it possible for them to focus on the long-term. In December 2010, Vook raised $5.25 million in Series A financing. Investors in this round included Vantage Point Venture Partners and FLOODGATE. Vook acquired Byliner, a digital imprint, in 2014.

They most likely will offer optional paid services or tools in the future. Right now, they're focused on their core publishing services, which they say will remain free. When you sign up for a Pronoun.com account, you are asked to verify through another site called https://www.medium.com. Here is the rundown, as far as we can determine.

- **Eligibility:** Persons age 13 and older
- **Exclusive:** Yes!
- **Reach:** Distributes to the five major retailers — Amazon, Barnes & Noble, Apple, Kobo and Google Play. Claims to reach 95% of the e-book market.
- **Key Restrictions:** Production tools are free, but their free ISBN numbers are eligible for use only as long as you distribute through them. Also, you cannot distribute to these five channels as long as you work with Pronoun.com, but you can distribute to other channels. We question whether submitting to some other sales channels might cause a conflict with the major retailers. This site does not take responsibility for any editorial inaccuracy. That's up to you. So be aware that a sales channel to which they distribute can reject your content if there are too many mistakes.
- **Royalty Rates:** pays 100% of the *net* income from a sale, after credit card processing fees and taxes.

CHAPTER 5

Subscription Services

A new kind of distribution scheme is based on **subscription services** and requires users to pay a monthly fee for the unlimited reading of books and audiobooks in their vast libraries. The top three purveyors of this arrangement were Scribd, Oyster, and Amazon Prime — Amazon being the biggest proponent. However, Oyster Books went belly up in early 2016, underscoring the doubtful effectiveness of subscription models for authors. We will discuss this in more detail later.

In the subscription model, the author is paid by being a member of a pool, much like a tips pool used by waiters or car wash personnel. At the end of the day or month, contributors divvy up what's been placed by customers in the kitty. However, for the author, there is a catch. He or she gets to participate in the pool only when and if a certain percentage of their book is read. If a subscriber downloads your book and only reads three or four pages, you may earn a few cents or nothing at all. That's very different than the traditional sales model, where the consumer buys your whole book, and it's up to them whether they read it or not.

Even if you make the grade in readership, the amount of money you will earn from a pooled sale may not amount to much. Earnings depend on how many other authors are in the pool with you at that time and how well each of their books has been read. Before we look at potential earnings in this model, let's visit the top players in the subscription arena.

As mentioned, Oyster Books —once touted as "the Netflix for books" — shut down in early 2016 after only a few years in operation. Rumors said that some of the Oyster team would move to Google, leading some to speculate that Google might set up a subscription service of its own. But sources at Google have denied any immediate plans for an e-book subscription service. The two remaining majors in this market are Scribd and Amazon.

Scribd claims to "pay the author the full price of their work," but they go on to say that revenues earned by the service from monthly subscriptions are paid to original publishers and authors "based on the agreements we have with them."

Here are some of the program's features.

Scribd[32]

- **Eligibility:** Adults
- **Exclusive?** No. Scribd has no direct author portal. You must use a third-party publishing partner, such as Smashwords or INScribe Digital, BookBaby or Draft2Digital
- **Reach:** 80 million readers in 100 countries (Source: Wikipedia — questionable stats)
- **Royalty rate:** See Smashwords for royalty rate. A sale only occurs if a subscriber reads more than 30% of the book, or browses 15%–30%. The author is paid the third-party royalty rate, not the Scribed Direct rate.

Scribd Direct[33]

- **Eligibility:** Adults
- **Reach:** You can upload content directly to the Scribd store, rather than through a third party.

---

[32] https://www.scribd.com/
[33] https://www.scribd.com/publishers

- **Royalty Rate:** Store charges author 20% + .25 transaction fee. The author keeps about 80% of list price.

TIP: *You may be better off to go direct than via the third party.*

Amazon Global Select Fund[34]

The Amazon Global Select Fund is a royalty pool through which authors are paid only for the number of pages read from a massive free shopping service called Amazon Global Select. The content (among other items) is offered free to Amazon Prime members. Members of Amazon Prime pay an annual fee of $99 to join to get free shipping, free content, and other perks. When you check one tiny box during the author sign-up process at the Kindle publishing site, you have automatically signed up for the 70% royalty plan.

- **Exclusive?** Yes! You can't sell anywhere else, not even your site. The KDP Global Select plan automatically forces you into **Kindle Owners Lending Library** (KOLL) and **Amazon Kindle Unlimited** (KU) subscription program for **Amazon Prime** subscribers — like it or not.

---

[34] https://kdp.amazon.com/select

TIP: *Watch what boxes you click on sign-up! You could be giving away more rights than you intended.*

- **Note:** When people borrow a book from the Kindle library or subscribe to Amazon Prime (unlimited reading), you DON'T get 70% of the sale! You could get zero, depending on how many pages consumers read and how many other books were in the pool and read that month. All you get is the "opportunity" to share in a small percentage of the pool. We'll explain later. See more details of how the program works in Chapter 6.

PART II

CHAPTER 6

Why the Amazon Subscription Program Is Not Your Friend

Amazon's Literary History and Philosophy

Amazon's greedy management philosophy has earned it the nickname, "evil enterprise" (Sources: ZDNet; *The Next Web; Digital Book World*). When Amazon has a beef with publishers and authors over pricing and terms, the company resorts to nasty tactics. They refuse pre-orders on books by claiming they are "unavailable," refuse to discount the prices of certain titles, slow the delivery of a publisher's books, and even suggest on some authors' pages that readers might prefer a different book.

Amazon's strategies may directly impact your marketplace visibility and your income. As Amazon's e-book market share rises, big publishers have seen their markets shrinking. (See www.Authorearnings.com). The average price of an e-book from the Big Five traditional publishers dropped from $10.31 in

January 2016 to $8.67 in May 2016, according to Authorearnings.com[35].The five majors are: Hachette Book Group, HarperCollins, MacMillan Publishing, Penguin Random House, and Simon & Schuster.

Author royalties decline as retail prices decline. Numerous bestselling authors who have seen incomes drop 20% or more in recent years, blame Amazon's predatory pricing strategies and misinformed court rulings. Independent authors, as we shall see, also can be affected.

Big name writers aren't the only ones who can be affected. So can you.

Understanding a bit of the company's history and philosophy can help you protect your work.

In 2010, the company owned 90% of the e-book market, according to *The New York Times*. The near-monopoly was temporarily thwarted that year with the introduction of iPad and a change in large publishers' pricing models, which later were ruled illegal by short-sighted federal courts. Today, at about 60- to 65% of the e-book market, Amazon is again poised to dominate the e-book market totally.

---

[35] http://authorearnings.com/big-five-may-2016-ebook-pricing/

Amazon is obsessed with controlling content — all of it, if possible. The company grabs exclusive rights to huge amounts of author content without laying down a dime. The content authors such as you freely give them (usually on an exclusive basis) is then used as a "come on" to sell Amazon's own lucrative subscription services for other goods and services. Amazon doesn't make much money from selling books. They are selling hard, physical products with much greater profit margins than books, and they are making a killing on shipping, often folded into subscription fees, or added on as premium services.

Amazon has two royalty plans for paying authors. One appears to pay way more than the other. But does it? On Amazon's seemingly high-paying 70% plan — in contrast to its 35% plan — Amazon gets exclusive rights to sell and loan your book on its retail site.

The company entices authors (especially self-published ones) to sign on to its "exclusive" and supposedly higher paying plan by giving the author the opportunity to share in a $12-to $15 million royalty pool. Once hooked into the program, you can't sell your book through any other retailer unless you break the contract. If you do decline, there is a three-month waiting period before you can offer the title for sale elsewhere.

The fund is heavily promoted to authors as a Holy Grail, and most everyone assumes that millions of dollars are shelled out every month to the lucky content providers. But the retailer does not disclose what is actually paid out to authors. The fund fluctuates from month to month. One assumes that all of the money for any given month is swept into authors' pockets, and that Amazon creates a new, even more lucrative fund next month. But there is no clear evidence of such a sweeping payouts.

What appears to earn the company some of the biggest bucks is the $99 per year fee that "Prime" subscribers pay for unlimited access to your book and other stuff — at no additional cost to them.

The promise of "free" shipping and other perks entices consumers; the "promise" of big royalties entices authors. No one is allowed to look behind the smoke and mirrors to see what Amazon paid to the people who write and produce the books.

The more content Amazon scoops up without paying, the less money authors will earn for their work and the fewer sales outlets they will have for their wares.

Again, Amazon's aim does not appear to sell authors' books; it is to own the market on an ever-expanding variety of products and services. Books serve as carrots.

How is Amazon going about achieving the ambitious goal of dominating the market for content?

First Step: Sell at a Loss to Grab Market Share and Kill Competition

The independent investment research firm, Morningstar, reported that Amazon's net profit margin[36] fell from 3.8% in 2009 to .56% in 2015, and may drop further in the coming few years. The drop in profitability appears to be a well-calculated move. Many believe the company deliberately cut its profitability to gain market share, drive out the competition and deter any newcomers from entering the market.

Amazon's ruthless price cuts have already driven out competitors such as Target and Wal-Mart, both of whom have pulled Amazon electronic reading devices from their shelves.

It appears that among the retailer's next targets is the traditional publishing industry itself, including the big five — Penguin Random House, Macmillan, Simon & Schuster, Hachette, and HarperCollins.

The problem with having a monopoly hold sway over almost all content is that Goliath can raise prices and change terms any

---

[36] http://financials.morningstar.com/ratios/r.html?t=AMZN

time it wants; this giant can decide who the winners and losers will be.

The publicly traded company claims that it is a champion of the consumer, lowering prices for everyone on just about everything — from games to groceries. In the short term, that may be true but at what price?

Why should you, the author, care?

In time, Amazon may erode your earnings, limit your book's availability in the marketplace and dictate whatever terms for your content it feels like applying. It could also largely control the availability of what people read.

The proof lies in the numbers.

Understanding How We Got Here

Before we draw a new picture of Amazon, let's explore a bit of history. Amazon began its subtle takeover of the publishing industry in about 2010. The move frightened the traditional publishing industry. Amazon had been taking a book that retailed for $12.99 and selling it at a $3 loss for $9.99 to drive out competition. The move destroyed the traditional "wholesale pricing model" that had been in effect for many years. In this model a retailer such as Amazon usually buys a book from the distributor or publisher for a 45-55% discount off the retail price. Amazon would buy the $12.99 book at 55% off — paying $5.84 for an item it would sell for $9.99 — but could have sold for $12.99. A mathematic example will make this scenario clearer.

Retail price: $12.99
Wholesale price: $5.84
Profit at $12.99 price: $7.15
Reduced Retail price: $9.99
Wholesale price (based on $12.99): $5.84
Profit at the lower price: $4.06
Lost profit: $3.09

While Amazon lowered the price of many books to $9.99, they cleverly continued to pay their authors the same royalty as they would have earned on a $12.99 book. So who'd complain? Had Amazon chosen to compute author royalties correctly on the $9.99 price, income would have suddenly dropped by about a dollar per sale.

Now, since Amazon has forced down the prices on all books, especially higher-priced bestsellers, author earnings have seen a significant drop. Some say earnings have declined as much as 50% or more.

Authors didn't immediately suffer because Amazon continued paying royalties on the original retail price of, say, $12.99. But traditional publishers foresaw the eventual lowering of all prices and thus the decline of profits for both themselves and their authors. Over time, authors would be making less money because of downward price pressures on all publishers. Amazon could decide at any moment to pay, not by a $12.99 book, but royalties based on a $9.99 book. Paying authors on the full $12.99 price would not last long as Amazon took a loss to gain market share.

Macmillan, the fifth largest book publisher, was first to attempt to bring more equitable terms to the table and proposed certain changes in its selling structure with Amazon. The giant retailer responded with a ruthless attack. Amazon exercised what is now known as its "nuclear option." The retailer promptly deleted the "buy" buttons in the Amazon online store for all of Macmillan's books. In an instant, Macmillan's entire business was in jeopardy.

The same thing can happen to you today.

In early 2010, a natural market solution to Amazon's power grab was born when Apple introduced its iPad into the e-book market. Apple suggested to the major book publishers that they change their e-book business model to reflect how Apple had been selling its popular apps for the iPhone. Under the app model, the publisher sets the price, not Apple or Amazon. The then-proposed new model moved pricing competition away from the e-retailers and into the hands of book publishers and authors, where many thought it should remain. Under that scenario, the retailers would keep a 30% commission. Apple met with five major publishers to offer them the new deal.

Faced with that universal pricing model, Amazon could no longer sell e-books at below cost. Also, the company's rivals had begun competing on service, spurring new entrants to the market and releasing innovative e-book devices. Publishes had blocked Amazon's goal of total e-book market domination

The company moved to eliminate the threat to their plans for market domination.

In April 2012, the Justice Department alleged that pricing of iPad digital books by the publishers was illegal collusion. The five publishers facing Justice Department action were Simon & Schuster Inc., a unit of CBS Corp; Lagardere SCA's Hachette Book Group; Pearson Plc's Penguin Group (USA); Macmillan, a unit of Verlagsgruppe Georg von Holtzbrinck GmbH; and HarperCollins Publishers Inc., a unit of News Corp.

As columnist Bob Kohn later pointed out in *The New York*

Times[37], "All was well until the Justice Department, supported by a white paper supplied to it by Amazon, filed an ill-advised lawsuit against Apple and five of the major book publishers for antitrust violations. The publishers were charged with 'price fixing' — but not for fixing prices: Not a single e-book price was fixed by the conspiracy contrived by the government. All the publishers did was to move to the lawful app store model, which eliminated Amazon's self-serving distortion of the e-book market."

Five months later, a federal judge approved a settlement[38] between the Justice Department and three of the five top publishers. The others had settled earlier. All this occurred despite protests from hundreds of parties including Barnes & Noble, the Authors Guild, and the American Booksellers Association. The ruling by Denise Cote, the federal district judge in Manhattan overseeing the case, empowered Amazon to drop the price of many e-books back to $9.99 or lower, pressuring competing retailers to do the same.

Publishers and authors predicted — and rightly so — that in the long run, the settlement could allow the e-book marketplace to

---

[37] http://www.nytimes.com/2014/05/31/opinion/how-book-publishers-can-beat-amazon.html?_r=0
[38] http://www.seattletimes.com/business/judge-approves-e-book-case-in-amazons-favor/

return to its state several years ago when Amazon held 90 percent of the market and other retailers struggled to get a foothold.

"I think that everybody competing with Amazon in the e-book market had better fasten their seat belts," said Mike Shatzkin, chief executive of Idea Logical, a consultant to publishers at the time. "I would expect Amazon to be leading the charge to cut prices on the most high-profile e-books. As soon as that starts to happen, all the books that are competing with them will have to reconsider their prices."

At the time of the settlement, Gina Talamona, a Justice Department spokeswoman, praised the ruling, saying "consumers will start to benefit from the restored competition in this important industry."

Statistics prove otherwise.

Competition has not been restored. Instead, Amazon is well on its way to becoming a monopoly in the e-book marketplace, as we shall see in a recent publishing industry sales report listed later in this chapter.

Effect on You as an Author

For authors, a monopoly is not a good thing. Some reports show that those who actually produce the content are making less money than they ever have as a direct result of the court ruling, which favored the giant retailer. And consumers are severely limited on their sources of content. The dominant publisher of books will soon be Amazon. Amazon — a near single source — may be in a position to say *which* books get published by the company's growing imprints and *which one's don't*. Amazon could decide which books get "buy" buttons or "read" buttons. Amazon could determine the size of the author royalty pool. Amazon will determine how those royalties get "shared" or not shared.

The big five publishers and other smaller presses are struggling to compete against the giant, which gobbles up most content free. Unaware authors sign exclusive agreements with Amazon and hand over their manuscripts to the media giant hoping to earn royalties from big sales which never materialize. Meanwhile, the outlets where authors can sell books continue to shrivel.

Is this the result the consumer (and the courts) wanted for the privilege of saving $3 on the price of a book or two?

The Daily Beast reported: David Young[39], the then chairperson and CEO of Hachette, told *The New Yorker*'s Ken Auletta, "The big concern — and it's a massive concern — is the $9.99 pricing point. If it's allowed to take hold in the consumer's mind that a book is worth ten bucks, to my mind its game over for this business."

As the Author's Guild then-head Scott Turow said upon hearing the court ruling in April 2012: "The irony of this bites hard: our government may be on the verge of killing real competition to save the appearance of competition. This would be tragic for all of us who value books and the culture they support." (Source: Melville Books website).[40]

The nuclear option against Macmillan — a catalyst for the lawsuit — was exercised for only a few days, a mere flexing of Amazon's muscles, according to a lawyer and *The New York Times* [41]columnist Bob Kohn. But imagine what would have happened if it had continued — and if it happened to you?

---

[39] http://www.thedailybeast.com/articles/2012/04/11/amazon-is-the-big-winner-in-justice-dept-suit-against-apple-and-5-publishers.html
[40] http://www.mhpbooks.com/how-do-you-respond-when-the-government-not-only-protects-a-monopoly-but-prosecutes-its-opponents/
[41] http://www.nytimes.com/2014/05/31/opinion/nocera-amazons-bullying-tactics.html?_r=3

"If you are wondering why Amazon would subject its customers to this inconvenience and wish to understand what's really happening between Amazon and Hachette — and, indeed, all the major book publishers — you need to know the meaning of the word *monopsony*," Bob Kohn wrote.

What Is a Monopsony?

"The Supreme Court Justice Sonia Sotomayor, when sitting on a lower court, once described monopsony as the 'mirror image' of **monopoly**. Unlike a monopoly, which occurs when a seller of goods has the power to unlawfully raise prices of what it *sells*, a **monopsony** occurs when a buyer of goods has the power to unlawfully lower the prices of what it *buys*. Each violates antitrust laws: As the Supreme Court has long recognized, they both result in a misallocation of resources that harms consumers and distorts markets," Kohn explained.

"With a major publisher such as Macmillan out of the market for new manuscripts, authors would receive less money. And less money would mean fewer authors and fewer books. (Nor are self-published authors safe from the power of a monopsony)," Kohn said.

He continued:

"The monopsony power of Amazon, which has a current market share of about 60-to 65 percent of all online book units, digital, and print, is not just theoretical; it's real and formidable.

"While a traditional publisher like Macmillan needs an author's consent to change the terms of his or her publishing agreement, Amazon reserves the right to change any provision of its agreement with any author at any time for any reason.

"How did Amazon attain such monopsony power? By providing valuable services? Perhaps to some extent. But consider that from the moment it introduced its Kindle product, Amazon sold e-books at prices far below what it was buying them for. If Amazon bought an e-book from Hachette for $13, it resold it to a consumer for $9.99, losing $3.01 per e-book. It should come as no surprise that under these circumstances, e-book buyers flocked to Amazon.

"But there was a problem. When a company has dominant market power and sells goods for below marginal cost, it is engaging in predatory pricing, a violation of federal antitrust laws."

Unfortunately, the publishers never had their day in court. Buckling under the expense and risk of antitrust litigation, they settled and agreed to restrictions clearing the way for Amazon to resume many of its practices.

We are reminded of the famous case, ***Standard Oil Co. of New Jersey v. the United States, 221 U.S. (1911)***[42]. The Supreme Court of the United States found Standard Oil guilty of monopolizing the petroleum industry through a series of abusive and anticompetitive actions.

Standard Oil allegedly used its size and clout to undercut competitors in a number of ways that were considered "anti-competitive," including underpricing and threats to suppliers and distributors who did business with Standard's competitors.

Over a period of decades, the Standard Oil Company of New Jersey had bought up virtually all of the oil refining[43] companies in the United States. By 1870, Standard Oil was producing about 10% of the United States output of refined oil[44]. Output quickly increased to 20% through the elimination of competitors in the Cleveland area.

---

[42] https://en.wikipedia.org/wiki/Standard_Oil_of_New_Jersey
[43] https://en.wikipedia.org/wiki/Oil_refining
[44] https://en.wikipedia.org/wiki/Standard_Oil_Co._of_New_Jersey_v._United_States#cite_note-1

The government sought to prosecute Standard Oil under the Sherman Antitrust Act[45]

The Court first had to decide if it had the power to regulate Standard Oil under the Commerce Clause[46]. Based on this review, the Court decided that the term "restraint of trade" had come to refer to a contract that resulted in "monopoly or its consequences" and ultimately concluded that Standard Oil's behavior went beyond the limits of the rule of reason[47] in the case.

According to The Daily Beast[48], here is how the case against Apple and the five publishers evolved:

> "Under a 'wholesale pricing model,' Amazon had been ordering e-books[49] for about $13 and selling them at a discounted rate of $9.99, taking a loss to get customers to buy other stuff, like the Kindle. When Walmart took on Amazon in 2009 and the two repeatedly marked down the prices of bestsellers — hard, physical book copies — they were able to get away with it also because

---

[45] https://en.wikipedia.org/wiki/Sherman_Antitrust_Act
[46] https://en.wikipedia.org/wiki/Commerce_Clause
[47] https://en.wikipedia.org/wiki/Rule_of_reason
[48] http://www.thedailybeast.com/articles/2012/04/11/amazon-is-the-big-winner-in-justice-dept-suit-against-apple-and-5-publishers.html
[49] http://www.thedailybeast.com/content/dailybeast/articles/2012/04/05/pew-e-book-survey-20-percent-of-u-s-is-reading-electronically.html

Walmart's real motive was to lure people online to sell them more expensive products.

"Apple didn't want to get into a price war with Amazon. For one thing, it didn't need cheap books to entice readers into buying iPads — the product was doing just fine. Instead, Apple reportedly convinced five of the six big publishing conglomerates (Penguin, Simon and Schuster, HarperCollins, Macmillan, Hachette) to set up an 'agency model' for e-book sales. It offered to allow the publishers to set whatever price they want, as long as Apple got a 30 percent commission. And because publishers had to offer the same contract to all 'like' retailers (Apple and Amazon), the big five asked Amazon to take it or leave it; Amazon balked at first, but ultimately took it."

That is why most e-books cost $12.99 at that point, and publishers and bookstores rejoiced.

The problem was that if Apple and the publishers did agree to set a price, this was illegal. So, the Justice Department filed the civil antitrust case against the five publishers, charging them with collusion and fixing the prices of digital books.

Just five months later, a federal judge approved a settlement between the Justice Department and three of the five major publishers over the objections of hundreds of parties, including the American Booksellers Association, the Authors Guild and Barnes and Noble.

The ruling by Denise Cote, the federal district judge in Manhattan, empowered Amazon to drop the price of many e-books back to $9.99 or lower and pressured competing retailers to do the same.

The result: Effectively, the Court once again cleared the way for Amazon to dominate the e-book market. But in this case, dominance in the e-book market does not necessarily mean more sales for the authors.

> "It feels like the Justice Department is solving a mythical problem and creating a bigger predator in this way," said digital content strategist Joe Wikert[50] of the ruling favoring Amazon. "If the settlement allows Amazon to return to its $9.99 model, the brand — most importantly, the author's name — would be cheapened."

And so it seems to have come to pass.

For Amazon the outcome was its first big victory, but not the only one.

---

[50] http://jwikert.typepad.com/the_average_joe/

Apple, Inc. appealed the ruling against it and the publishers. But, in March 2016, the Supreme Court refused to hear its challenge to the collusion case. Thus, the decision by The Second U.S. Circuit Court of Appeals in New York stands. Apple was ordered to pay $400 million to consumers who "overpaid" as well as another $50 million to cover challengers' legal fees. The final blow to Apple meant a victory for Amazon, clearing the way once again for Amazon to dominate the e-book market.

Impact on the Traditional Publishing Industry

In the years following the 2012 ruling, fissures in the health of the traditional publishing market have widened.

In September 2015, the largest U.S. trade association for the publishing industry, the **Association of American Publishers (AAP)**, reported that what was regarded by the media as a flat US e-book market was the result of a shrinking market share among traditional publishers. Here is how the AAP characterized the state of the traditional publishing industry:

> "In the 18 months between February 2014 and September 2015, the AAP, whose 1200 members include the 'Big Five': Penguin Random House, HarperCollins, Simon &

Schuster, Macmillan, and Hachette — saw their collective share of the US e-book market collapse:

- from 45% of all Kindle books sold down to 32%
- from 64% of Kindle publisher gross dollar revenue down to 50%
- from 48% of all Kindle author net dollar earnings down to 32%

The AAP releases monthly StatShot reports on the total dollar sales of their 1200 participating publishers, of which the 'Big Five' collectively account for roughly 80%.

The AAP's reports for 2015 (most recent report at press time) have charted a progressive decline in both e-book sales and overall revenue for the AAP's member publishers."

During that same period in 2015, Amazon's overall e-book sales have continued to grow in both unit and dollar terms, fueled by a strong shift in consumer e-book purchasing behavior away from traditionally published e-books and toward indie- published and Amazon-imprint-published e-books. Since author royalties are based on pages read (in the 70% royalty plan), increases in sales do not necessarily reflect increases in royalties.

These "non-traditionally-published" books now make up nearly 60% of all Kindle e-books purchased in the US and take in 40% of all consumer dollars spent on those e-books.

Many authors — self-published or otherwise — are feeling steep declines in income.

The AAP report as of May 2015 had not taken into account the latest 5% drop in their collective market share, measured by Author Earnings in early September 2015 (after Penguin Random House's return to agency pricing; thus setting its own pricing).

Large publishers are losing ground to Amazon's plans for becoming the nation's super publisher using a monopsony. And no one is stopping them.

A team of researchers at Macmillan's offices in New York City continually sifts through a database of 74 million book sales transactions looking for trends. Amazon looms large in the findings. In September 2015, the giant retailer accounted for 64% of the U.S. e-book market, by units sold, during the second quarter, according to Codex (Source: *The Wall Street Journal*, September 3, 2015)

Even so, signing an exclusive contract with Amazon to reach the Kindle market may be short-sighted. The millions of dollars Amazon advertises as a pool for author royalties may reach the wallets of only a few well-known authors. Meanwhile, authors on the 70% royalty plan have signed away their work for little or nothing.

For you as a self-published author, and perhaps for many other authors, more money might be made by staying independent. You can simply choose Amazon's 35% royalty deal instead of the seemingly lucrative 70% plan. You can also opt out of the Prime program, sticking with the regular sale of your book. The choice will free you to sell across all markets, and still distribute to Amazon through the lower royalty plan.

Authors and Booksellers Now Demand a Justice Department Antitrust Inquiry

Five years after Amazon secretly asked regulators to investigate the five publishers for price fixing, thousands of authors, agents, and independent booksellers are retaliating. They have banned together to ask the **U. S. Justice Department**[51] to examine Amazon for antitrust violations.

---

[51] http://www.nytimes.com/interactive/2015/07/13/business/document-authors-guild-investigate-

The group includes The Authors Guild, the American Booksellers Association, the Association of Authors' Representatives and Authors United, according to a *New York Times* report by David Streitfeld[52].

The American Booksellers Association and the Authors Guild have rarely united in such a fashion, but they said they increasingly realized that their fates are joined. The booksellers have about 2,200 stores. The guild has 9,000 members. Most members are published through the traditional publishers who count on the stores to display their new titles and create interest in them.

Douglas Preston, a Hachette writer and an influential Amazon detractor instigated the current call for government inquiry with the support of Authors United[53], an international collaboration of authors from different backgrounds, thought groups, ages, languages, and cultures.

---

amazon.html?rref=collection%2Ftimestopic%2FJustice%20Department%2C%20U.S.&action=click&contentCollection=timestopics&region=stream&module=stream_unit&version=search&contentPlacement=3&pgtype=collection
[52] http://topics.nytimes.com/top/reference/timestopics/people/s/david_streitfeld/index.html
[53] http://authorsunited.net/

In letters and statements[54] sent to the Justice Department, the group charged that "Amazon has used its dominance in ways that we believe harm the interests of America's readers, impoverish the book industry as a whole, damage the careers of (and generate fear among) many authors and impede the free flow of ideas in our society.

"Disruption is healthy, an inevitable byproduct of a world that changes," Mr. Preston told *The Times*. "But there isn't a single example in American history where the concentration of power in one company has, in the long run, benefited consumers."

Critics charge that in recent years Amazon has engaged in content control, "selling some books, but not others, based on the author's prominence or the book's political leanings"; selling some books below cost as loss leaders to drive less well-capitalized retailers — like Borders — out of business; blocking and curtailing the sale of "millions of books by thousands of authors" to pressure publishers for better deals.

In a 24-page position paper[55], Mr. Preston laid out his case, together with Barry C. Lynn, a senior fellow at the New America

---

[54] http://www.nytimes.com/interactive/2015/07/13/business/amazon-authors-united-documents.html
[55] http://www.nytimes.com/interactive/2015/07/13/business/document-amazon-book-practices.html

Foundation and author of "Cornered: The New Monopoly Capitalism and the Economics of Destruction."

Douglas Preston, at the shack he uses as his writing space in Pemaquid, Me. He has emerged as an influential Amazon detractor with his group Authors United. Photo *with permission: Doug Preston*

The groups said they had tried to interest the Justice Department in Amazon before, without success.

European regulators recently said they, too, were beginning an antitrust investigation into whether Amazon[56] used its dominant position in the region's e-books market to favor its products over rivals.

---

[56] http://topics.nytimes.com/top/news/business/companies/
amazon_inc/index.html?inline=nyt-org

The **European Commission**[57] is evaluating the legality of clauses that Amazon used with European publishers, which required them to inform the e-commerce giant when they offered more favorable terms for books to other digital retailers. Since Amazon is by far the most powerful e-book retailer, such clauses might prevent an innovator from breaking through, according to *The New York Times*. The **European Commission** (EC) is the executive body of the European Union responsible for proposing legislation, implementing decisions, upholding the EUtreaties and managing the day-to-day business of the EU.

In America, Apple and the publishers involved in the Justice Department case argued that whatever the short-term effect on consumers, the entry of another major participant (namely Apple and the five publishing houses) would provide more competition and thus benefit consumers in the long term.

As we now know, the publishers settled the case out of court. Apple lost at trial, lost again in June 2015 on appeal and yet again when the Supreme Court refused to hear its case in March 2016.

---

[57] http://topics.nytimes.com/top/reference/timestopics/organizations/e/european_commission/index.html?inline=nyt-org

"Antitrust for the last 30 to 40 years has focused on economics — the price that someone pays for something," said Michael Carrier, an antitrust expert at Rutgers School of Law in Camden, N.J. in a *Times* article. "It is an ill-fitting tool to address concerns about a company's effects on culture."

One indication of the tough road Amazon's critics have is that the Justice Department official in charge of the antitrust division, William J. Baer[58], in 2016, celebrated Amazon's "disruptive business model" in e-books, saying it "has continued to stoke competition."

Peter Meyers, author of "Breaking the Page"[59], a new book about the shift from print to screen, disagreed, saying "Amazon's success has quashed competition" in e-books.

"Sure, there are the subscription services, Oyster [now defunct] and Scribd, but those businesses aren't really robust yet," said Mr. Meyers. "More meaningful is the cratering of Barnes & Noble as a competitor."

---

[58] http://www.justice.gov/opa/speech/assistant-attorney-general-bill-baer-delivers-remarks-chatham-house-annual-antitrust
[59] http://www.amazon.com/dp/B00PQ83VD4/ref=cm_sw_su_dp

CHAPTER 7

How Amazon Global Select Works

Let's look at how Amazon Select works (or doesn't) for the author.

First, a few definitions.

Kindle Prime: a user subscription program in which a person pays $99 a year to get unlimited reading, free shipping and other perks from Amazon. Amazon is pushing the Prime (unlimited reading) program to become bigger, most likely because it makes the company more money and enables it to gobble up exclusive content for free.

- People get FREE looks at your book while you earn almost nothing.
- It takes a ton of partial/full reads to get paid anything at all because your book is included in a huge pool of other books with which you must share royalties.
- Each free library read is potentially one less regular sale on Amazon or any other vendor since the program blocks you from selling your book anyplace else.

Kindle Unlimited (KU): Prime subscribers get the opportunity to read as many books as they like without paying anything additionally.

Kindle Owners Lending Library: Kindle owners with Amazon Prime memberships can choose from thousands of books to read for free once a month from the Kindle Owners' Lending Library (KOLL) which is currently available to Amazon Prime customers in the U.S., UK, Germany, France, and Japan. KOLL is different from the Lending for Kindle feature, which allows readers to lend digital books to their friends and family after buying them on the Amazon.com Kindle Store. See more details about payments from the Global Fund for the lending library here[60].

Kindle Select: This plan opts the author into Amazon's subscription program, automatically placing the author's title in the unlimited reading pool, as well as its lending library, thus enrolling them in KDP Select Global Fund.

KDP Select Global Fund: The author payout for this pool of funds once was based on a straight percentage of your book that was read, divided among all books read that month. As of the summer of 2015, that has changed. Amazon has conjured

---

[60] https://kdp.amazon.com/help?query=lending+library

up a complicated algorithm to determine how you get paid out of the pool. It's called Kindle Edition Normalized Pages (KENP) Read, which supposedly accurately calculates exactly how many pages a consumer read for the first time. Your author payment is determined based on the number of pages read from your book, based on your "share of total pages" read (up to a total of 3,000 pages per customer per title) by all Kindle Unlimited (KU) and Kindle Owners' Lending Library (KOLL) customers. The share of funds allocated to each country varies based on a number of factors such as exchange rates, customer reading behaviors, and local subscription prices.

Kindle Edition Normalized Page Count (KENPC v2.0):

The KENPC is used to determine how much of your book was read by a user. To determine a book's page count, the **Kindle Edition Normalized Page Count (KENPC)** is calculated using standard formatting settings (font, line height, line spacing, etc.) to measure the number of pages customers read in your book, starting with the Start Reading Location (SRL) to the end of your book. Amazon typically sets SRL at chapter 1 so readers can start reading the core content of your book as soon as they open it. Non-text elements within books including images, charts, and graphs will count toward a book's KENPC.

The new KENPC approach is applied uniformly to all KDP Select books and all versions of those books. No matter which version a customer may be reading, all future royalties will be paid using KENPC v2.0. If a customer previously borrowed your book and is still reading it, any new pages read will be based on KENPC v2.0. Extremely long books, such as dictionaries, are also calculated on the same basis, up to a maximum of 3,000 KENPC pages.

In your Kindle account's Sales Dashboard, you can see total pages read. Amazon says, "Because it's based on default settings, KENPC v2.0 may vary from page counts listed on your Amazon detail page, which are derived from other sources."

Hm-m-m. So the page count on your Dashboard doesn't balance with the public information that shows on your detail page of the Amazon site. Why? Could this be an attempt to inflate how popular your book is to entice more readers while paying you on a smaller count?

Amazon claims the total payout from the KDP Select Global Fund "has been unaffected by the transition" to KENPC v2.0, and the amount you earn from the global fund will continue to be determined based on your share of total pages read by Kindle Unlimited (KU) and Kindle Owners' Lending Library (KOLL) customers. Amazon claims that the new KENPC system hasn't affected author royalties. Since Amazon won't tell us how much they are paying to authors, we can't prove this claim one way or the other.

A system with per-page payouts is a system that rewards cliffhangers and mysteries, rewarding anything that keeps people hooked, the Atlantic[61] has observed.

"While many larger publishers' offerings are included in these programs, the details of those deals have not been made public. Their authors may or may not be paid by the page. The new formula applies to Kindle Select books that are self-published and distributed through Amazon's Kindle Direct Publishing program," the report pointed out.

---

[61] http://www.theatlantic.com/business/archive/2015/06/amazon-publishing-authors-payment-writing/396269/

CHAPTER 8

What Is the True Earning Potential of Amazon Select?

The first barrier to your earning potential within the Amazon Select program is author visibility. The size of the pool of FREE content is so large (more than a million titles, half or more of which are self-published) that being discovered on the site poses a real problem without massive (and costly) marketing promotion — in particular for the new author with little name recognition.

If a customer indeed locates a book anywhere on the web and actually buys it for $9.99, they are much more likely to read the whole thing and buy the author's next work, than if it's a freebie through their Prime subscription. The consumer isn't as likely to toss it aside for millions of other free books if he/she has invested the money to read it.

If you display your book for sale on an independent website such as, say, Kobo Books[62], we might assume the title is more

---

[62] http://www.kobobooks.com/

likely to be found and purchased than if found among the millions of free titles on Kindle.

The second barrier to your earning potential at Amazon may lie in the author payment pool itself, where the competition for actual readership is intense.

How much can you expect to earn in royalties if your book is part of the Amazon Global Select program? And if it is such a good deal, how come Amazon applies its new "pages read" formula only to Kindle Select books that are self-published and distributed through Amazon's Kindle Direct Publishing program, rather than to all authors in its publishing programs?

Since most authors now only get paid from the royalty pool, Amazon may be paying out small change when compared to what they used to pay. They have the authors ensnared. They no longer have to pay them anything unless a portion of their books, that are accessible for free are actually read.

Amazon's Example of Earnings

Amazon Kindle gives some rather ludicrous examples of an author's potential earnings from the Select Fund.

The example is calculated based on a $10 million fund with 100,000,000 total pages read in the month. They even admit that the scenarios are "extremely optimistic." Here are the calculations, according to Amazon:

- The author of a 100-page book that was borrowed and read completely 100 times would earn $1,000 ($10 million multiplied by 10,000 pages for this author divided by 100,000,000 total pages read by everyone that month).
- The author of a 200-page book that was borrowed and read completely 100 times would earn $2,000 ($10 million multiplied by 20,000 pages for this author divided by 100,000,000 total pages read).
- The author of a 200-page book that was borrowed 100 times but only read halfway through on average would earn $1,000 ($10 million multiplied by 10,000 pages for this author divided by 100,000,000 total pages).

Realism or hype?

When broken down to its lowest denominator, earning potential becomes apparent. If the 100-page book were read only one time that month the author would earn 0.00001 — a mere fraction of a cent. (That is, 100 pages divided by 100,000,000 total pages read).

If the same author were to sell that single book under the regular 70% plan at the average sale price of $9.99, they would earn $6.99.

There is a good reason why we should question Amazon's examples. Amazon does not report how many actual pages are read by subscribers, so it is impossible to verify what portion of the exemplary $10 million pool gets paid out.

The Kindle Unlimited market itself is highly competitive, with 1.3M books vying for a share of the approximately $15M monthly Global Fund (as of 2016).

Many author forums are already reporting that only a few pages of their books if any, are read, and they are lucky if even one book is borrowed or bought in a single month. Later we will see comments from some real life authors enrolled in the Select program.

Self-Published Authors' Average Annual Earnings

To test the viability of Amazon's example, let's look at average author earnings. The following statistics are not meant to frighten you away from a writing career. Rather, the numbers can give you a stronger picture of just how viable Amazon may be for the self-published author. Armed with more knowledge you will be able to make better choices for placing your books into effective sales channels.

According to **Digital Book World**, 65% of self-published authors in recent years have made less than $4,999, based on a survey of 5,000 authors. Earnings amount to about $416 per month in book sales. At an average price of $6.49 ($2.99-$9.99), you'd earn $4.54 per sale ($6.49 x 70% royalty), and would need to sell approximately 1100 books over a 12-month period on Amazon to earn that average income.

Another survey[63] by *Digital Book World* and *Writer's Digest* later found that 54% of "traditionally published" authors (and nearly 80% of self-published authors) earn less than $1,000 a year.

PublishingPerspectives.com[64] reported that "Just over 77% of self-published writers make $1,000 a year…with a startlingly high 53.9% of traditionally-published authors, and 43.6% of hybrid authors, reporting their earnings are below the same threshold. Only 0.7% of self-published writers, 1.3% of

---

[63] http://publishingperspectives.com/2014/01/how-much-do-writers-earn-less-than-you-think/#.V2HFkPkrLIU
[64] http://publishingperspectives.com/2014/01/how-much-do-writers-earn-less-than-you-think/#.V2HKpfkrLIV

traditionally published writers, and 5.7% of hybrid writers reported earning more than $100,000 a year from their writing."

A May 2016 article by Author Earnings[65] found that the Big Five publishers' most-heavily-promoted frontlist launches were still largely in the $12.99–$14.99 range. But once you move past that visible tip of the iceberg, a broader look at the prices of all 157,000 Big Five e-books in the May dataset revealed a significant shift. The average price of a Big Five e-book had dropped from $10.31 in January 2016 to $8.67 in May 2016

Author Earnings said that a key point it made in its recent *Digital Book World* presentation[66] was that "higher e-book prices end up hurting newer debut authors far more than they hurt long-established authors, who already have existing fan bases and sustainable writing careers — especially those perennial bestsellers who have managed to become household names." The data offered "clear indications that, between 2014 and 2016, higher prices had progressively damaged the earnings of new Big Five debuts, and even more crucially, crippled their 'discoverability' — that all-important key to establishing the brand-new readership and fanbase necessary to establishing a long-term writing career."

---

[65] http://www.digitalbookworld.com/2016/author-earnings-new-report-on-big-five-ebook-pricing/
[66] http://authorearnings.com/2016-digital-book-world-presentation/

The triptych of slides in the presentation made that case with glaring starkness: in them, "we can see Big Five debut authors dropping from 22% of e-book sales in early 2014, down to barely 9% of those vital, career-launching initial sales in early 2016."

How Does Amazon's Promise of Big Earnings Measure Up?

Amazon tells you that you could earn $2,000 if your 200-page book is read just 100 times in a single month — nearly five times the statistical average of monthly author earnings, according to the *Digital Book World* surveys. Is this achievable? You decide.

In hard-to-find data, *Digital Book World* reported in January 2015 that Amazon Kindle's monthly individual author payout equaled **$1.38.**

Other subscription services are likely to be much less.

What Critics and Authors Have Said About Amazon Earnings

From leading publishing industry experts to individual self-published authors, the implications for success with Amazon's own publishing imprints have not appeared universally bright, even from the beginning, and throughout its publishing history.

Amazon Publishing launched its first imprint in 2009, targeting self-published authors, then expanded into full editing and book publishing in 2011, when it opened a publishing office in New York City. The idea was to compete directly with large publishers.

It was in New York, in fact, that Amazon Publishing "began to seem like a flop," according to a thoughtful article in Seattle Weekly, The Perks, Pitfalls, and Paradoxes of Amazon Publishing[67].

Although Amazon had at the time partnered with Houghton Mifflin Harcourt to release print versions of its titles, many bookstores simply wouldn't sell them. Barnes & Noble announced a boycott in January 2012, casting the move as a retaliatory strike against Amazon's actions in the e-book market. Amazon was pushing publishers, agents, and authors into making their titles available only on the Kindle, thus undermining Barnes & Noble's rival e-reader, the Nook. Other booksellers followed suit, angered in particular by a price-check app

---

[67] http://archive.seattleweekly.com/home/955189-129/the-perks-pitfalls-and-paradoxes-of

Amazon developed for the 2011 Christmas season which encouraged consumers to use stores as showrooms before buying online.

The bookstore ban affected Amazon Publishing's ability to sign up authors too.

For big name authors accustomed to seeing prominent stacks of their work in bookstores, Amazon's inability to get into stores was unappealing.

Even Amazon founder Jeff Bezos' wife MacKenzie, a novelist, picked Knopf Doubleday as her publisher for a new book released in 2013.

Most well-known authors who signed on to Amazon Publishing were unable to get on *The New York Times'* best-seller lists. The Times does not track e-books tracks E-Books available exclusively from a single vendor, presumably because the Times does not trust Amazon to report sales figures on its own titles without independent verification.

"Within a year of the New York office opening, Amazon decided that the original strategy was not going to work, according to the ex-staffer," the Seattle Weekly reported. "The new mandate: Forget big names. Forget bookstores. And refocus on the Kindle, both regarding publishing e-books and of skimming off the cream of writers self-publishing through Kindle Direct." In late 2014 self-published authors comprised about half of all books, Amazon acquired for publication, a figure that has no doubt risen within more recent years.

"It was difficult for me to understand what they were thinking," the *Seattle Weekly* quoted veteran New York agent Jane Dystel, daughter of a legendary publishing figure who once headed Bantam Books. Amid the churn of opening offices in New York came a lot of people "who didn't have traditional publishing experience," she said.

Amazon moves employees around so that a person hired for her film experience, for example, might end up marketing books or toasters or children's puzzles. For Dystel's clients, the outcome was mixed.

On the one hand, she told *Seattle Weekly*, some of the authors whose work she sold to Amazon have had an "extraordinary" experience. They include the London-based Helen Bryan, whose novel about romance during World War II, *War Brides*, was first published in Britain. Dystel estimated the book sold about 7,500 copies there. Amazon acquired and e-published the book in 2012. The marketing campaign, Dystel says, was "brilliant," entailing "lots of online promotion."

This strategy worked particularly well with *War Brides.* It sold over 500,000 copies.

"Dystel, though, has represented other authors who have had far less success with Amazon," the *Weekly* reported. "In such cases, the company's marketing methods fell flat. In its haste to get a lot of books out quickly, Amazon 'might not have understood the market,' she said. 'Or the market might not have been as easily defined.' And when that happened, Amazon let the data make its next decision: It passed on the author's next book.

"All publishers do this," Dystel acknowledges, "but they aren't usually so aggressive in seeking out authors, building them up, and then almost spitting them out."

"Meanwhile, the days of six-figure Amazon advances are gone. We're seeing advances somewhere in the range of $10,000 or $20,000."

"You might say those who even get an advance are lucky. Amazon relies on many authors to start their careers without any advance at all," Dystel told the newspaper.

Read the full report here[68].

More damning comments came in a much later article in *The New Yorker*[69], by George Packer. He wrote that nearly all of Amazon Publishing's books have under-performed.

Wikipedia reports from the Packer article that Amazon purchased two high-profile books at auction including Timothy Ferriss[70], The *4-Hour Chef*[71] for 1 million dollars, which did worse than his previous titles; and *My Mother Was Nuts*, a memoir by Penny Marshall[72], for eight-hundred thousand dollars, which only sold seventeen thousand copies. *Actors Anonymous*, a novel by James Franco[73], has sold fewer than five thousand copies. Packer said "In the past year, Amazon Publishing has barely been a presence at auctions, and several editors have departed; last month [January 2014], Kirshbaum left the company, having failed at the task Amazon gave him." Reasons given for the poor performance include bookstores which refuse to carry Amazon titles since Amazon is a direct competitor; incompetence as a publisher. As one New York

---

[68] http://archive.seattleweekly.com/home/955189-129/the-perks-pitfalls-and-paradoxes-of
[69] http://www.newyorker.com/magazine/2014/02/17/cheap-words
[70] https://en.wikipedia.org/wiki/Timothy_Ferriss
[71] https://en.wikipedia.org/wiki/The_4-Hour_Chef
[72] https://en.wikipedia.org/wiki/Penny_Marshall
[73] https://en.wikipedia.org/wiki/James_Franco

publisher said about Amazon, "There are certain things it takes to be a publisher. You have to have luck, but you also have to have judgment, discernment. Amazon's culture of machines, algorithms and mass products don't fit well with the publishing world's emphasis on human networking and reputation."

According to *Publishers Weekly*[74], Amazon Publishing may have scaled back its plans to have a major New York City trade publishing presence since the departure of Larry Kirshbaum a couple of years ago, but the company still continues to expand its overall publishing operation. The division is now composed of 14 imprints, based in six cities, and publishes about 1,200 titles in a year. Though it was largely focused on commercial fiction when it launched in 2009, Amazon Publishing is now increasing its investments in such nonfiction areas as narrative nonfiction, memoir, and biography, PW reported.

Criticism of Amazon's publishing tactics is rampant on the Internet, extending from publishing icons right now to individual self-published authors.

---

[74] http://www.publishersweekly.com/pw/by-topic/industry-news/publisher-news/article/66593-amazon-publishing-marches-on.html

Buzz in the Forums

A quick look at Internet forums indicates Amazon's poor earning power for the majority of self-published authors who give up their rights in the blinding light of marketing hype. Shortly after Amazon started the Kindle Edition Normalized Pages idea, there was a groundswell of reaction from authors. Here are a few forum comments:

Posts: 168
Registered: 02/12/15

And how many people are buying your 120 page book for $3.95. I write a series and each episode runs close to 120 pages on average. I sell each one for $1. So, I get 0.35 when I sell and I get about 0.70 (assuming 0.0058) when I lend it.

I would not pay what you are asking for a 120 page book for an unknown author, but I would love t know if you are being successful. I get more than three borrows for each sale so, from my perspective, lending appears to be more profitable. If I sold my works for $3.95 each and, I would break even at about one-eighth of current sales.

What are your sales to borrows ratios?

Edition Normalized Pages (KENP) Read?
Posted: Aug 1, 2015 4:35 AM in response to: Luca Montemagno   Reply

$0.0058 per page read is terrible. If I sell my 120 page book and make 70% or 2.77 per book that is 0.023 per page. We'll never make any money with this new KENP system. Something is wrong here.

Blue
Orbiter
Co...

Re: How much for the Kindle Edition Normalized Pages (KENP) Read?
Posted: Aug 1, 2015 6:51 AM in response to: tom ward   Reply

Re: How much for the Kindle Edition Normalized Pages (KENP) Read?
Posted: Aug 1, 2015 6:52 AM in response to: tom ward Reply

Actually you were getting a great deal before at the expense of those who wrote longer works.

Edited by: Blue Orbiter Corporation on Aug 1, 2015 6:53 AM

Re: How much for the Kindle Edition Normalized Pages (KENP) Read?
Posted: Aug 1, 2015 11:37 AM in response to: Blue Orbiter Co... Reply

Just LIL but based on the hypothetical half-a-cent-plus projection, my estimate is about triple the royalties over the 'books borrowed' format.

I ran a kindle advertising campaign and spent almost all the $100 allocated but still lost a bit of money. The ad was for the first in a two book series (volume three is nearing completion).. Don't know whether the campaign resulted in borrows or not but extrapolating the page numbers for the two into books read, the numbers compare about the same as units borrowed in previous months.

I'm pleased to see it appears both volumes are being read cover to cover with the second volume lagging behind the first by a couple thousand pages for July.
I also have a teaser sample that is 88 pages and was borrowed exactly once with 65 pages read. Don't know whether that reader read most and then tossed it aside or just couldn't wait to get into the whole thing. I've noticed reviews seem to have dropped off. Wonder if readers don't think they should review something they didn't pay for. Only four reviews in the past year that weren't verified purchases so I assume these were borrows

Several enlightening comments appear on the Reedsy blog[75] in an item titled, "What authors actually think of Amazon's Pay-Per-Page Model." One respondent wrote:

> "Overall, authors who wrote full-length novels were actually getting screwed. If I'd wanted to game the system, I should have focused on writing five 20,000 words stories (earning $6.60 if all are borrowed) rather than one 100,000 page book (earning only $1.32 if borrowed). Under Kindle Unlimited my income would have been five times what it is. Under the new system, my income is more, as long as those pages get read." — Bob Mayer[76] author of the Area 51[77] series

How Does Readership Equate With Author Earnings?

Chris McMullen[78], author of *A Detailed Guide to Self-Publishing with Amazon and Other Online Booksellers* follows author payments, and Kindle reading estimates on his blog, He

[75] https://blog.reedsy.com/amazon-pay-per-page-model
[76] https://writeitforward.wordpress.com/2015/07/02/yes-once-more-amazon-is-screwing-authors-set-to-pay-them-006-per-page/
[77] http://www.amazon.com/Area-51-Book-ebook/dp/B0083X4VXI/ref=sr_1_1?s=digital-text&ie=UTF8&qid=1437495646&sr=1-1&keywords=bob+mayer+area+51
[78] http://amazon.com/author/chrismcmullen

reported the Kindle Unlimited per-page royalty rate held steady at $0.00477885 for March 2016. It's nearly identical to the $0.00479 for February 2016.

Both February and March were up considerably (about 17%) over January's rate of $0.00411.

Ordinarily, the Global Fund increases when the per-page rate decreases, and the Global Fund decreases when the per-page rate increases but seems to be holding relatively steady. Find more details on his blog[79].

In other words, when readership drops, Amazon ups the size of the Global fund, one presumes because they aren't paying out as much. But who really knows. An increase in the fund looks good as a marketing angle.

According to McMullen, the average KDP Select book earns about $11 per month from borrows ($15M divided by 1.3M books), though hardly any books draw in this exact average. The top books, the KDP Select All-Stars, see a million or more pages read in many cases.

McMullen says that if your book gets over 2300 pages read per month, it's doing better than the average KDP Select book.

---

[79] https://chrismcmullen.wordpress.com/tag/kdp-select-global-fund/

(That's how many pages read it takes to earn the average $11 per month.)

McMullen indicates we are on a downward trend with respect to page rates.

"If the per-page rate drops too much, down to whatever your magic number is, the question you need to ask is whether you can do better outside of KDP Select than you can inside. It's not an easy question to answer, and it varies from one author and even one book to the next. (Keep in mind that every borrow helps your sales rank, which is one thing you'll lose if you switch to the other side.)

"We haven't reached my magic number yet. But I wouldn't mind if we didn't dip below $0.004…

"On the other hand, it started at $0.0058 back in July, and now it's 29% less, down to $0.0041. I sure would like to see it stop going down…," he concluded.

How Much Money Does Amazon Actually Share With Authors?

To formulate a guess as to how generous Amazon is with authors, we need to consider what the company is earning from its Prime membership program.

While Amazon does not release Prime membership numbers, Consumer Intelligence Research Partners, LLC (CIRP) regularly analyzes buyer shopping patterns on the site to make its own well-educated guess as to how many there are.

"This analysis indicates that Amazon Prime now has 54 million U.S. members, spending on average about $1,100 per year (not necessarily on books), compared to about $600 per year for non-members," the research company said in a press release[80] that looked at Q4 of 2015. This new estimate compares to an estimated 40 million U.S. members at the end of 2015, or an increase of 35%, according to previous CIRP figures. (Source: *The Motley Fool*[81])

The ruthlessness with which Amazon beats down its competition can be seen in the Association of American Publishers report on authorearnings.com[82]

Let's pull together some hard-to-find statistics to build a hypothetical model of how Amazon is cheating authors.

---

[80] http://files.ctctcdn.com/150f9af2201/ae0b58e0-f4a5-4d83-916b-ec0757dc95db.pdf
[81] http://www.fool.com/investing/general/2016/01/26/how-many-prime-members-does-amazon-have-and-why-it.aspx
[82] http://authorearnings.com/report/september-2015-author-earnings-report/

- Kindle's overall inventory = 1 million Kindle books (according to its website[83]). Who knows how many are shared from the library, or accessed via Prime?
- 54 million users subscribe to Prime. Not all are readers. (Source: The Motley Fool[84])

Let's do a little math to see who is making money here — you or Amazon? Multiply 54 million subscribers times $99 and you get roughly $54 million in annual income just from subscription fees, excluding any other sales and revenues from shipping.

- Kindle sales= $265,000,000 (Latest reliable source: Forbes Magazine April 2, 2014-Estimating Kindle E-Book Sales for Amazon.[85] The figure is probably much higher now.
- Kindle Digital Publishing Select Global Fund (February 2016) =$12 million.
- Estimated percentage of sales paid to authors: 3-4%
- Estimated amount Amazon keeps for itself: about $253 million ($265,000,000 less $12,000,000 in the Global Fund. And this does not count $54 million in subscriber fees.

---

[83] https://www.amazon.com/gp/kindle/ku/sign-up/ref=kbhp_nb_ku
[84] http://www.fool.com/investing/general/2016/01/26/how-many-prime-members-does-amazon-have-and-why-it.aspx
[85] http://www.forbes.com/sites/greatspeculations/2014/04/02/estimating-kindle-e-book-sales-for-amazon/#180104755bfc

How Much Would Amazon Have Paid Authors on a Straight Sale?

Using the estimated total revenues of $265,000,000 (million) in our earlier scenario, divided by an average book sale of $9.99 would mean they would have sold 26.6 million books in a year under the traditional sales model.

Consider 26.6 million books x 70% royalty means they would have paid out $18.5 million in author royalties under the traditional sales model. But under the pool, they are only laying aside about $12 million in escrow for authors. Even if they did pay out 100% of the pool, they would add another $6.5 million ($18.5 million-$12 million) to their own pockets under the pool system vs. traditional book sales.

To summarize:

$265,000,000 in Kindle e-book sales
+$54,000,000 from Prime subscriptions
=$319 million income
Less $12 million in author payouts (or escrow)
Amazon's Total take: $307 million

Note: Before Amazon switched its payment method to an author pool, the company's reported author pool totaled $13,250,000. So the amount paid to authors has declined by more than a million dollars after applying the new reading algorithm, called Kindle Normalized Page Count (KNPC).

How Much Is Amazon Making With Its Prime Program?

Keep in mind Amazon is earning $99 per year from about 20 million Prime subscribers. That's $19.8 million (and climbing) from subscription fees alone.

Prime members read some or all, of your book FREE. So who's making money here? Authors or Amazon?

Grabbing Author Content for Free

Because Amazon advertises that a huge pile of money is "available" to authors who sign up for their exclusive program says nothing about how much authors are earning from the pool. Amazon is only required to shell out "if" pages are read by an algorithm they designed. And they refuse to disclose those total readership figures. The public impression, however, is that authors are cleaning up on works sold through the Amazon pool. Who has seen evidence that the bulk of those funds ever reaches the authors?

We Asked Amazon to Clarify Payouts; They Wouldn't

Since Amazon refuses to release the actual amount paid to authors, there is no way to tell. In March 2016, as part of our early research for this book, we asked Amazon's public relations department to answer these questions:

1. How many book titles do you offer in the Kindle Unlimited catalog?
2. How many authors are enrolled in the Kindle Select program?
3. On average, how many total pages are read each month in the Kindle Unlimited catalog?
4. Of the advertised $12 million annual author royalty pool offered to Amazon Select authors (or $1 million per month), what is the average collective monthly payout to authors?
5. Within the past 18-24 months, has there been any increase or decrease in the amount of money offered in this fund? If so, what are those changes and are they in any way the effect of your new Kindle Edition Normalized Page Count (KENPC) system?

6. Do the bestselling Direct Publishing authors participate in the same Global Select fund or are they paid differently? If so, on what basis are they paid?

Here is their response,
dated Tue 3/22/2016 4:57 PM:

Hi Doris,

It's Justin O'Kelly in the PR department at Amazon, Jennifer [Cooper] shared your inquiry with me and I apologize for the delay in getting back to you.

Some of the data you've asked for we do not share, but data regarding the size of pool is public knowledge:

    December 2014 - $7,250,000

    January 2015 - $8,500,000

    February 2015 - $8,000,000

    March 2015 - $9,300,000

    April - $9,800,000

    May 2015 - $10,800,000

    June 2015 - $11,300,000

    July 2015 - $11,500,000

    August 2015 - $11,800,000

    September 2015 - $12,000,000

    October 2015 - $12,400,000

    November 2015 - $12,700,000

    December 2015 - $13,500,000

    January 2016 - $15,000,000

February 2015(sic, actually 2016) - $14,000,000

The amount authors earn from the global fund is determined based on their share of total pages read by Kindle Unlimited (KU) and Kindle Owners' Lending Library (KOLL) customers.

For more on the fund, please see these links:
https://kdp.amazon.com/select
https://kdp.amazon.com/help?topicId=AI3QMVN4FMTXJ

Justin

Thus, there is no clarity or certainty in Amazon's exclusive deal. Terms can change anytime. The fluctuations from month to month are also unexplained and do not necessarily reflect amounts paid out.

Kindle Publishing is Different Than Kindle Digital Publishing

Kindle's Digital Publishing (KDP) program is not the same as receiving an actual Kindle Publishing contract with Amazon. If you are lucky enough to get a real publishing contract from Amazon — the traditional kind — here is a little of what you can expect, according to the company's Kindle Scout Agreement[86]. Kindle Scout is reader-powered publishing for new, never-

---

[86] https://kindlescout.amazon.com/agreement

before-published books, where readers supposedly help decide if a book gets published. Selected books will be published by Kindle Press and receive 5-year renewable terms, a $1,500 advance, 50% E-Book royalty rate, easy rights reversions and featured Amazon marketing. If the author does not earn at least $25,000 in royalties during any of those five years, they can request their rights back, known in the industry as "reversion." If the author earns less than $500 in a two-year period from the title's release date, they can also request a reversion or Amazon itself may decide to revert your rights if sales are poor.

Guess who gets to set the sale price of the book? Amazon. They also do not pay you for any promotional copies, samples or excerpts of your work. Here's what they say on their site:

> "**Net Revenue** means, for each format or edition of your Work, the gross amounts we actually receive from the sale of copies of that format or edition, fewer customer returns, digital transmission costs and bad debt, and excluding taxes. Net Revenue for your Work from participation in a subscription or other blended fee program will be determined in accordance with the standard revenue allocation methods for that program that are applicable to Kindle Press books.

> **Royalty Table**

E-book:	50% of Net Revenue
Digital Audio:	25% of Net Revenue
Translation in e-book format:	20% of Net Revenue

You can submit your book for consideration here:
https://kindlescout.amazon.com/submit

What Are You Giving Up
or Away with Amazon EXCLUSIVITY?[87]

As quoted on the Amazon site, "all content included in or made available through any Amazon Service, such as text, graphics, logos, button icons, images, audio clips, digital downloads, data compilations and software is the property of Amazon or its content suppliers and protected by United States and international copyright laws. The compilation of all content included in or made available through any Amazon Service is the exclusive property of Amazon and protected by U.S. and international copyright."

We hope you make the most effective decisions in distributing your e-book.

---

[87] https://www.amazon.com/gp/help/customer/display.html/
ref=s9_acss_ft_ki_x_column3_link1?nodeId=508088&pf_rd_m=ATVPDKIKX
0DER&pf_rd_s=center-3&pf_rd_r=MMD1MYP77XKN4TTDY916&pf_rd_t
=1401&pf_rd_p=2391456882&pf_rd_i=1000664761

CHAPTER 9

Getting Started

on the Self-Distribution Journey

To begin your distribution journey, here are a few points to remember:

- Pick a strategy: Go direct via publisher portal, or hire distributor?
- Make a written pricing and distribution plan. What are your target outlets?
- Study each sales channel's restrictions to figure the greatest return.

TIP: *Think before making a book FREE on one sales channel. It will apply to all.*

- Try to sell one book at each of 3,000 retail outlets per month to earn a reasonable living. Assume a profit of $2 per book x 3000 = $6,000 x 12 months =$72,000/ year.
- If one retailer owns 60% + of the market, you're missing the other 40%.
- Beware of subscription models. They may not be so good for you.

- Beware of retailers' termination clauses and price restrictions. They impact your earnings.
- Study an outlet's audience reach before devising a plan.
- Read the fine print; identify the "gotcha's."
- Remember, "easy" and "free" don't always achieve the best possible results.
- Think small. Where are the independent booksellers? What retailers offer the best access to them? Check out the Independent Book Publishers Association (IBPA)[88].
- Go for the greatest possible number of sales outlets, not necessarily the largest.
- Have realistic expectations about how many books you will sell.
- Go nonexclusive. Don't limit your reach in a changing market.

A few important marketing outlets

- Facebook, Twitter, Reddit, Pinterest, Imgur, YouTube
- Top 15 blogs: http://www.ebizmba.com/articles/blogs
- Top 15 top online news outlets: http://www.ebizmba.com/articles/news- websites

---

[88] http://www.ibpa-online.org/

- The Independent Book Publishers Association (IBPA) provides several effective ways to market your books.
  - Cooperative mailings
  - Trade show exhibits
  - Catalog mailings

Don't ignore newspapers

- Study shows, don't ignore newspapers yet!
- US daily newspapers = about 1380
- Digital audience up 17% over 2013 to 166 million visitors
- 80% of US adults online engaged with digital newspaper content
- 91% of women 25– 34 were reached by digital media that month
- Mobile-only access to newspaper content up by 85% over last year; young women (18– 24) up by 173%

Source: Newspaper Association of America, study

Now, go for it! Wishing you every success.

Quick Comparison of Major E-Book Retailers' Royalty Plans

Check all websites for updates. Also read notes below for clarification. Be aware of whether you are being paid on the basis of net income or gross income!

List Price	Amazon.com**** USA (See notes below)	BN.com	Apple iBook store	Ingram Spark* (Publisher sets price)	Kobo**
0.99-$2.99	35% Non-exclusive. File size restrictions apply.	40%	70%	40% (45% excluding Kindle)	38%-60%
$2.99-$9.99	35% Non-exclusive; 70% exclusive + delivery costs.	65%	70%	40% (45% excluding Kindle)	38%-60% 60%/list; 70.05%/ net $ from affiliates
$10-$199.99	35% Non-exclusive; 70% exclusive + delivery costs. File size restrictions may apply.	40%	70%	40% (45% excluding Kindle)	38%-60% 60%/list; 70.05%/ net $ from affiliates
.99-12.99	35% Non-exclusive, minimum price varies on file size; 70% exclusive from $2.99 minimum + delivery costs.	40%	70%	40-45%	38%-60% 60%/list; 70.05%/ net $ from affiliates
$12.99+	35% Non-exclusive; 70% exclusive + delivery costs	40%	70%	40-45%	38%-60% 60%/list; 70.05%/ net $ from affiliates

Big Aggregators

Smashwords ***	Scribd Store direct. Pub Acct. Sub price: $8.99	Scribd Subscription for Self-pub		Other Retailers
60%/list; 70.05%/net $ from affiliates	80%, less .25 cent/ trans fee, each download	Via Smashwords paid only if 30%+ of book is read.		40%-55%
60%/list; 70.05%/net $ from affiliates	80%, less .25 cent/ trans fee, each download	via Smashwords paid only if 30%+ of book is read.		40%-55%
60%/list; 70.05%/net $ from affiliates	80%, less .25 cent/ trans fee, each download	via Smashwords paid only if 30%+ of book is read.		NA
60%/list; 70.05%/net $ from affiliates	80%, less .25 cent/ trans fee, each download	via Smashwords paid only if 30%+ of book is read.		40%-55%

Notes

*Ingram Spark royalty is 40% with Kindle; 45% without; print ranges between 45%-70% + $25 setup fee.

**Kobo rate is 60% based on list price in US/CA only; 38% for other outside territories. Affiliate sales earn 70.05% of the net income.

*** Smashwords pays only quarterly; most others pay monthly.

****In the USA, Amazon restricts sale prices based on the size of your e-book file. If your file size is greater than 3 MB, you can sell your book for a price between $1.99 and $200. If your file size is greater than 10 MB, the lowest you can price the item is $2.99 (and no greater than $200). If you price your book lower than $1.99, your file size cannot exceed 3 MB. Check Amazon for updates on restrictions. 70% plan adds delivery charges; 35% plan does not. VAT taxes added to overseas markets. See complete Amazon pricing here: https://kdp.amazon.com/help?topicId=A29FL26OKE7R7B

Index of Terms

(Linked to definitions in the book)

W

X

About the Author

Doris Booth founded Authorlink in 1996 after having headed her own successful advertising and marketing agency serving Fortune 1000 companies such as the high-tech organization, SAP America. Earlier in her career, she served as an award-winning newspaper editor and journalist. She was the youngest editor in the State of Texas to head a division of a major newspaper chain. Later she served as public relations coordinator for the then Chairman of the U.S. House Ethics Committee and the House Science and Technology Committee. She has long been on the leading edge of technology and was among the first to embrace print-on-demand and e-book publishing. As editor-in-chief of Authorlink she has overseen the conversion of more than 200 e-books, and has edited, published and marketed many titles. She continues to represent a small, closed group of successful authors and has lectured for a number of writing organizations, including the Whidbey Island MFA Writing Program and the Independent Book Publishers Association (IBPA).

For more information

Authorlink.com

Doris Booth

dbooth@authorlink.com

972 402-0101

www.ingramcontent.com/pod-product-compliance
Lightning Source LLC
Chambersburg PA
CBHW031126020426
42333CB00012B/250